Insight and Social Betterment

Insight and Social Betterment

A Preface to Applied Social Science

JAMES B. RULE
State University of New York, Stony Brook

New York
OXFORD UNIVERSITY PRESS
1978

Printed in the United States of America

Library of Congress Cataloging in Publication Data

Rule, James B   1943-
   Insight and social betterment.

   1. Social problems.   2. Social sciences—Method-
ology.   3. Social policy.   4. United States—Social
conditions—1960-   I. Title.
HN18.R78   309.1'73   77-27277
ISBN 0-19-502392-7
ISBN 0-19-502393-5 pbk.

To my parents,
Calvin Rule
Ruth L. Rule

Preface

This book is about the relationship between the study of social conditions and effective steps to improve them. It is not, however, a book of practical instructions; it does not provide advice such as how to perform evaluation studies or how to organize consciousness-raising. Instead, the book examines some issues which ought to be entertained before undertaking such concrete activities. These include such fundamental questions as the meaning of social betterment, the extent of social change which it is reasonable to expect and plan for, the role of "expert advice" in official policy *versus* grass-roots political action, and the contribution of social science inquiry to all of these things. All of these discussions have to do with one underlying concern—that of whether better understanding of social life can help bring about what people might acknowledge as "improvement" in social conditions; and if so, how.

My own interest in these issues grew out of the social and political ferment of the late 1960's and early 1970's in America. That period fostered an intensification of concern with the study of social, political and economic conditions as the key to their improvement. The peculiar thing, it seemed to me, was that every contending social and political viewpoint had its own interpretation of the proper relationship between better understanding and the attainment of a "better world."

Nor were any of these interpretations wholly persuasive in themselves. In certain government and academic circles, for example, there developed an almost fanatical profession of belief in the official use of social science advice. Yet a close look at the actual behavior of working politicians and bureaucrats suggested something different: They seemed not to base their political and administrative decisions on research, so much as to select research to justify political and administrative requirements. On the other side of the political fence, dissident intellectuals and activists often insisted on "correct" political and social analysis as essential to fruitful action. But their thinking often seemed to embody so many controversial assumptions that its effect was only on those already converted.

As the turbulence abated in the mid-1970's, people were asking why social science had not provided the expected "answers." Yet a close look at the period made it plain that the expectations of social science themselves had been confused and mutually inconsistent. This book, written mostly between 1974 and 1977, attempts to go at some of these questions more thoroughly.

Although the impulse to begin this work sprang from the current events of a particular period, the study has forced me to concentrate on very old issues in the history of social thought. In fact, these are fundamental contextual issues both for my own discipline, sociology, and for other social science fields. Naturally I hope that these pages will contribute to scholarly discussion in these fields.

But I also hope that this book will reach thoughtful people outside the universities. "Applied" social scientists, as well as academic ones, should find much here to speak to their concerns. Indeed, people in all sorts of government and private bodies are in the position of sponsoring social change, whether they think of their work in these terms or not. They, too, will be concerned with making such change as "rational" as possible, and I hope that they will find this book useful in that connection.

Many institutions have provided essential support for my efforts in writing this book. One very important body is my academic home, the Sociology Department at the State University of New York, Stony Brook. Another is Nuffield College, Oxford, where this book was conceived and where I spent a very pleasant summer working on it during 1975. That summer research was sponsored by a NATO Senior Science Fellowship awarded by the National Science Foundation. The last year of the writing has been funded mainly by a Rockefeller Foundation Humanities Fellowship. *Politics and Society* and *The American Journal of Sociology* have kindly granted permission to reprint, in revised form, Chapters One and Two, respectively. The last few weeks of the writing have been completed at the Center for Advanced Study in the Behavioral Sciences at Stanford, under funding from the Guggenheim Foundation and National Science Foundation grant BNS–76–22943. I am acutely aware how directly my ability to carry out this work has depended on the backing and encouragement of these agencies, and I wish to record my sincere gratitude to all of them.

Some special thanks are in order to the Rockefeller Foundation, whose Humanities Fellowship freed me from a year's teaching responsibilities, during which time the book has been completed. Everyone close to the social sciences these days knows that money currently available for research is overwhelmingly for "applied" activities. This means, in effect, research to help organizations accomplish purposes already fixed through the elephantine processes of bureaucratic decision making. Little backing, strangely enough, goes to studies like this one, which raise questions about the *setting* of such purposes or, *horribile dictu*, about the underlying assumptions on the use of knowledge in society. At a historical juncture where grotesque overemphasis has been placed on such "applied" research, Rockefeller have moved in a different direct-tion. They have been able to fund studies which ask not how we may streamline our "progress" in the current direction, but whether we really want to make the trip in the first place. Even within the protected world of private foundations, such efforts are rare and deserve special acknowledgment.

In addition to all of this fine institutional support, many friends and colleagues have contributed crucial advice and encouragement. Particularly important have been those who have tried to educate me to schools of thought or to ideas which I needed to understand but which began by being "foreign territory" to me. Certainly it is no fault of theirs that I have been unwilling or unable to take all of their good advice. These people include Lewis Coser, Forrest Dill, Jean Floud, Tony Giddens, John Goldthorpe, A. H. Halsey, David Held, Paget Henry, George Homans, Dick Howard, Thomas Luckmann, Michael Mann, Ruth Meyler, Jozef Niznik, Mancur Olson, Terry Rosenberg, W. G. Runciman, Theda Skocpol, Paul Streeten, and a number of others. In addition, James Anderson of Oxford University Press has provided essential help and encouragement, and Frances Campani has supplied all sorts of moral, intellectual and procedural support in the closing months of the work. My sincerest thanks to all of them.

Finally, some special thanks to my good friend and distinguished colleague, Lewis Coser. Without his goading, encouragement, criticism and advice this book could not have been written. A colleague like this is simply priceless.

J.R.

Stanford, California
October 1977

Contents

Insight and Social Betterment

Introduction

Does better understanding of social conditions lead to their improvement? Can we expect the study of such things as social conflicts, public opinion, political parties, social movements, bureaucracies and whole societies to help bring about a better world? For many people, the response to such questions may be surprise that they could even be asked. We live, after all, in a rationalistic age. We are accustomed to regard all forms of scientific inquiry not only as worthwhile ends in themselves but also as rich sources of practical benefit.

This faith, as applied to social science, shapes both the thinking of social scientists and public expectations of their work. The turbulence of American society in the late 1960's and early 1970's yielded a bumper crop of appeals for studies of troubled social conditions, as steps toward their amelioration. Indeed, we may have passed the point of satiation with pronouncements like the following:

> We are living in social crisis. There have been riots in our cities and in our universities. An unwanted war defies efforts

to end it. Population expansion threatens to overwhelm our
social institutions. Our advanced technology can destroy natural beauty and pollute the environment if we do not control
its development and thus its effects. . . .

At the root of many of these crises are perplexing problems
of human behavior and relationships. The behavioral and social sciences . . . can help us survive current crisies and avoid
them in the future. . . .[1]

Clearly, social science has come to share the prestige of natural
science as a force for social betterment. Even when the study of
social conditions does not immediately secure the improvements
that people desire, optimism remains unabated. People attribute
such failure to the youthful underdevelopment of the social sciences or to the inadequacy of resources allocated for action on social science recommendations. Questioning the underlying principle of the inherent beneficence of social science does not come
naturally.

And yet, there are many circumstances which ought to encourage such questioning. For one thing, we have grossly discrepant
accounts of how the beneficial effects of social science should come
about. The same period of public controversy in America which
gave rise to the appeals for official problem-solving efforts described above also yielded other, contradictory claims. These demands had it that social scientists should use their special position
for a frontal attack on the political establishment. The proper role
of the social scientist, in this view, was that of the aggressive, informed public advocate. This challenge provoked a vigorous response from the social science establishment. Philip Hauser, a former president of the American Sociological Association, entered
the following counterattack against those he labeled "actionists"
in the discipline:

[1] National Academy of Sciences, *The Behavioral and Social Sciences:
Outlook and Needs* (Englewood Cliffs, N.J.: Prentice-Hall, Inc., 1969),
p. 1.

By eschewing political action as a professional and scientific body the association would by no means be failing to contribute to the resolution of the acute and chronic problems which afflict this nation and the entire world. This would no more be the case than the refusal of the biochemist engaged in cancer research to treat a cancer patient. Biochemical research may contribute more to the elimination of cancer in the longer run than will the biomedical engineer, the physician, who treats the cancerous patient. Similarly, the fund of knowledge produced by sociological research may contribute infinitely more to the solution of social problems than the disruptive and violent tactics of the New Left actionists. . . .[2]

Whatever one may think of Hauser's position, his strong words lay the matter squarely on the line: If the study of society is to help make social relations "more rational," what account can we give of how these effects are to take place? People's views on this subject vary remarkably according to their social position. For those close to the exercise of power—government planners, for example, and the experts who advise them—the usefulness of social inquiry lies in its potential to generate effective policy advice. Those estranged from power, on the other hand—the revolutionary, the community organizer, or the radical intellectual—seek the benefits of social inquiry more in its power to inform indictments of the status quo or to provide insights for the conquest of power. The seven chapters of this book review different interpretations of the role of understanding in the improvement of social conditions. What we will find is hardly consensus but rather a smorgasbord of often mutually contradictory strategies. The only constant is the contention that better understanding ought to help, somehow.

Nearly everyone involved in the study of society has his or her own ideas about the role of understanding in creating a

[2] Philip M. Hauser, "On Actionism in the Craft of Sociology," in J. David Colfax and Jack L. Roach, eds., *Radical Sociology* (New York: Basic Books, 1971), p. 437.

better world. Most people, I suspect, base their expectations on some favorite example of the practical fruitfulness of social science knowledge. Such a "success story"—where social inquiry has led to improved social planning, or more effective grass-roots organization, or the inspiration of some important political action —cements faith in the social usefulness of social science. "There," we may say. "*That* goes to show how beneficial our efforts can be."

But as the Yiddish saying has it, " 'For instance' is no proof." The "success" of social science insight in a particular setting, by the lights of a particular observer, hardly demonstrates its *general* utility. For this, we need some criterion of "success" or "social betterment" which other thoughtful observers could accept. And we need a detailed rationale as to how understanding can conduce, in the larger assessment, to these effects. These requirements demand some complex and subtle arguments.

Nonetheless, many people persist in discussing the relation between understanding of social conditions and their improvement as though it were about as straightforward as that between aspirin and headaches. One wonders why. Perhaps because this simplistic view embodies just a grain of truth. For understanding does confer real *instrumental* advantages in dealing with the social world. Just as the engineer must know as much as possible about his or her materials, the politician should know as much as possible about his or her constituency. Just as the surgeon seeks the best possible data on the patient's preoperative condition, the revolutionary will want the fullest information on the strengths and weaknesses of the regime to be subverted. When the goal is *manipulation* of the social environment, knowledge generally enhances the interests of the knower.

So far, so good. But the usefulness of social science in promoting *individual* interests may tell us rather little about its role in promoting some broader "public interest." For this larger public interest—whatever we may mean by the term—can hardly represent simply the sum of individual advantages. Access to a lawyer will improve the position of anyone involved in a legal tangle. But only the most naïve optimist would hold that a proliferation of lawyers would make society as a whole "more just."

Ordinary ways of talking often blur these distinctions and conceal the complexities involved. Indeed, the language of social science itself may distract attention from the conflictual nature of troubled social conditions. We often speak of "social problems," for example, as though they were conditions which everyone deplored. Yet most troublesome social conditions are not really "problematic" in this sense. Such conditions almost always involve oppositions of interest between two or more parties. They are problematic because what helps one party hurts the other, and because these antagonisms have unpleasant repercussions for the rest of society. What pass for "racial problems" in contemporary America are the symptoms of conflict between supporters and opponents of more privilege for blacks. The "problem" of pollution reflects a division of interest between those who especially profit from polluting activities and those who do not. Social science faces few authentic social problems, in the sense of conditions which hurt everyone equally. More often, problematic social conditions are those where help to one set of interests can only mean harm to others. How, then, can any form of insight conduce to betterment of society from some overall standpoint?

Any serious attempt to deal with such issues quickly evokes questions of ultimate value. And this means reckoning with Max Weber's famous arguments on this subject. For Weber, clashes of political viewpoints such as those implicated in many social problems entailed clashes of ultimate value. In other words, social groupings oppose one another in the name of opposing principles —e.g., equal rights for all citizens *versus* states' rights, or the right of every worker to a job *versus* the right of capitalists to dispose of resources as they see fit. Sociological analysis, Weber held, could help people understand the *implications* of their values—for example, by clarifying to the proponent of laissez-faire principles the likely consequences of their implementation. But the ultimate questions, say, of whether a social and economic order based on free enterprise is morally preferable to a benevolent, managed welfare state—these Weber saw as unanswerable through empirical analysis. Such questions he regarded as more matters of metaphysical taste than matters of evidence. Seeking "rational" decisions on questions like those cited above, Weber held, is about as promising as seeking rational bases for a choice between chocolate and vanilla. Thus, by implication, the prospects for "rational solutions" to social problems are not promising. One might as well attempt rational mediation between dogs and cats.

Confronted with such riddles and apparent contradictions, some may respond merely with a shrug. Perhaps, some would conclude, any overall assessment of the good or bad effects of social inquiry really is impossible. Perhaps one can do no more than identify notable positive or negative effects of particular inquiries. Thus, any verdict on the usefulness of social science "for society as a whole" would remain forever in abeyance.

Such a position need not be illogical. But those who take it must confront certain awkward realizations. First, even the most thoroughgoing skeptic in these respects would probably want to maintain that social inquiry at least does not produce results that are, on balance, downright harmful. And even this modest faith implies some sort of sociolgical calculation as to why it should be so. Second, such skepticism runs counter to claims of the social sciences for their present share of public resources. One reason for the relative favor presently enjoyed by social science is undoubtedly the supposition of its beneficial social influence. Members of these disciplines who doubt the social usefulness of their fields can probably be expected not to declare these doubts too loudly to the world at large.

In any event, those who have written most insightfully about the social role of social science have not often taken the skeptical position. They have generally tried to develop a rationale showing how some particular form of social inquiry can transcend the difficulties noted above. They have attempted to show, in other words, how a certain way of studying society can meet the "true" or "ultimate" needs of humankind or of society "as a whole." These formulae inevitably require serious sociological arguments in their own right. They demand assumptions about such matters as the propagation of ideas in society, the relation between ideas and action, the forces underlying social change, and a host of other eminently sociological concerns.

The seven chapters which follow examine some of the most influential arguments on these points. In the interest of concentrating on the *sociological* content of these arguments, these discussions slight certain important but non-empirical issues—e.g., the question of the *ultimate* nature of the "good society." Instead, I mean to struggle with questions such as the following: Given one writer's view of "social betterment," is it reasonable to expect others to orient their efforts to this same notion? Do the proposals for social inquiry advanced by a particular writer represent a plausible and coherent plan of scholarly action? And, perhaps most importantly, does the form of enhanced social understanding which the writer favors really promise to have the desired *effects?*

These seven chapters are separate essays, each of which stands on its own. Nevertheless, they develop a coherent approach to the dominant ways of thinking on these issues. Chapter One criticizes the influential technocratic or "social problem-solving" approach. This chapter opens a line of argument central to this book—the contention that any approach to "rational improvement" in social relations entails political content, overt or concealed. Chapter Two extends this critique of technocratic thinking to other approaches to rational social betterment. None of these approaches, I argue, wholly succeeds in ridding itself of partisan political content. Chapter Three examines the sociological content of political doctrines themselves. It attempts to specify to what extent, if at all, social science inquiry can lead to "rational" choice among contending political positions.

The next three chapters present further interpretations and criticisms of major approaches to these issues. Chapter Four deals with Karl Popper's influential arguments on the role of reason in "piecemeal social engineering." Chapter Five examines the contribution of the Frankfurt Tradition in Germany—the Critical Theorists and Jürgen Habermas. Chapter Six discusses the ideas of Gunnar Myrdal and Paul Streeten on the relationship of the social scientist to the shifting values and interests which form the context for his or her work. The seventh, final chapter attempts to bring these discussions together in some synthetic concluding statements.

The arguments examined here are all fresh, often even topical. And yet, the analysis of these ideas will involve us in controversies of very long standing. Most major figures in the history of social thought have attempted to show how their formulae for social inquiry should lead to the enrichment of social life. The arguments examined here thus all have lengthy intellectual pedigrees. Yet, all of these arguments will be found to leave important questions unanswered.

Again, we live in a rationalistic age. It goes against the grain to question the idea that extended understanding of social life should enrich it and help resolve its troubles. To doubt this assumption is to call into question the munificence of charitable foundations, the labors of countless government commissions of inquiry, and the *raison d'être* of numerous academic schools, departments, and disciplines. It is to cast doubt on the most fundamental impulse of the scholar: to respond to troubled social conditions by studying them.

Such questioning comes hard, then. Yet it is only fitting that critical inquiry should focus on the social effects of reason itself. The sociological judgments required in assessing the long-term, cumulative effects of social research and theorizing are indeed difficult. They will never afford the certainty of more exact forms of social inquiry. But not to attempt such judgments would be to ignore questions which are logically prior to the efforts both of working social scientists and of all others seeking reasoned attempts to improve social conditions.

The plan of this book—a series of critical essays on the most influential approaches to these contentious issues—is of a nature to arouse controversy. I am sure that practically nobody will agree with all the viewpoints put forward here, and some, no doubt, will take exception to nearly all of them. I welcome such controversy, and only hope that it will stimulate readers to sharpen their own positions on these matters. If we can agree that the questions involved are richly subtle and impossible to beg, that will be ample reward.

1

The Problem with Social Problems

During the late 1960's and early 1970's, everyone now agrees, America experienced a period of exceptional social conflict. This period was also marked by the unprecedented growth of participation in government policy making by outside "experts," and especially by academics from the social sciences. The two developments are obviously related. These social science experts served, above all, to help in formulating the official response to our troubled domestic situation.

One product of this symbiosis between social scientists and policy makers has been a distinctive way of talking about public issues. This synthesis of social science vocabulary and officialese now continues to suffuse public discourse outside the government, as well. The irony is that this language, despite the turbulent times of its origin, systematically obscures the bitter oppositions of interest which underlie major public issues in America. Race, pollution, poverty, the cities—all of these so-called "social problems" amount to contests over the control of desirable resources, including wealth, privilege, and, above all, political power. These issues turn on clashes of interest and thus represent *political* conflicts. And yet, in the language of collaboration between government and social science, they are treated instead as *social problems,* as forms of "social sickness." This unwarranted application of clinical language to politics is misleading and dangerous. For it suggests that political conflicts can somehow be resolved apolitically, through the dispassionate intervention of experts. And this suggestion paves the way, in turn, for the imposition of partisan measures in the guise of non-political "solutions" to "social problems."

TECHNOCRATIC PROBLEM-SOLVING

The most predictable occasion for the flourishing of this rhetoric is the proposal or inauguration of new ventures of cooperation between the federal government and professionals from the social sciences. Some such projects have envisioned very extensive participation by such experts in the creation and execution of government policy. One of the most sweeping was made by Dr. Nicholas Golovin, then of the President's Office of Science and Technology. He proposed nothing less than a fourth branch of government, composed of experts from the physical and social sciences, to provide advice and, presumably, consent to the three existing branches on matters of policy. In particular, the new agency would "a) collect all the data necessary to continually track the state of the nation, b) define potential problems suggested by the information, c) develop alternative plans to cope with the problems, and d) evaluate ongoing projects in terms of real time and advise the people accordingly."[1] John Lear, writing in *Saturday Review,* paraphrases John Gardner in expressing support of the proposal: "Everyone is talking about cleaning up the ghettos, modernizing transport, and

[1] John Lear, "Public Policy and the Study of Man," *Saturday Review* (September 7, 1968), p. 60.

making equal education available to all, but no one is working on a system of priorities for realization of those reforms or a fair distribution of the costs. In short, the current crisis in American society hinges on authoritative evaluation. . . ."[2]

The drift of these recommendations, and the assumptions they entail, must be familiar to anyone attentive to public discourse in America. Certainly one notes here the trademark of the rhetoric mentioned above—the notion that major public issues consist of "social problems" to be "solved" by the massive application of technical expertise. And on the face of things, the idea seems unassailably reasonable. Everyone knows that America faces grave "social problems"; one presumes that the more expert skill available for their solution, the better. But what is misleading and dangerous in these suggestions is the notion that these essentially political issues can be resolved by expertise alone, without introducing politics. For there can be no definition of a "social problem" which does not involve political judgments, nor certainly any "solution" to such problems devoid of partisan content. To pretend otherwise merely leads to the introduction of partisan measures in the guise of non-political, technocratic "problem solving."

Another case in point is the publication in 1969 of *Toward a Social Report*, by the Department of Health, Education, and Welfare. This hundred-page document was written by members of the Department staff after consultation with a blue-ribbon panel of eminent social scientists. It represents a lobbying effort aimed at the institution of a more exhaustive yearly social report consisting of an array of "social indicators" or statistics describing the "social health" of the nation. The authors define "social indicator" as ". . . a statistic of direct normative interest which facilitates concise, comprehensive and balanced judgments about the conditions of major aspects of a society. It is in all cases a direct measure of welfare and is subject to the interpretation that, if it changes in

---

[2] Ibid.

the 'right' direction, while other things remain equal, things have gotten better, or people are 'better off.' "[3]

Again, the idea seems beyond reproach; who, after all, could possibly be against "social health"? Yet, before long, it becomes apparent that the authors' idea of "social health" is hardly something that all of us could agree on, but a creature of their own highly partisan political views. For one of the "pathological conditions" which they deem worthy of documentation through social indicators is alienation. They write: "People need a sense of belonging, a feeling of community, in some small social group. If such associations are lacking, they will feel alienated; they will have a tendency either to 'cop out' of the central life of the society, or else try to reverse the direction of the society by extreme or even violent methods. The more numerous and stronger the social ties that bind an individual to the social order, the more likely he is to feel an attachment to the society, and work within existing rules to improve it."[4]

So, the desire to "reverse the direction of society by extreme or even violent methods" and the unwillingness to "work within existing rules to improve it" are manifestations of individual and social ill-health, according to these authors. But why not the other way around? Why not bracket those unwilling or unable to face up to the need for drastic social change in America as "sick"? Certainly, for anyone who mistrusts the intentions of those who hold power in America, and who sees little hope for improvement short of major changes in our basic political forms, disaffection from the present regime is reasonable and proper. Of course, the authors of *Toward a Social Report* do not share this critical view of American society, nor do the experts who advised them on the preparation of the booklet. But shouldn't they represent their political positions for what they are, instead of portraying them as received clinical truth?

[3] P. 97.
[4] P. 88.

POLITICAL MEDICINE

Such difficulties are endemic where essentially medical discourse is applied to political questions. The authors of *Toward a Social Report* talk about alienation much as one would talk about a disease—as something which no one could possibly favor—while quite ignoring matters of political context. For while no one may desire alienation as a good thing in itself, the feelings one has about the significance of alienation are tied to one's whole system of political values. If one sees popular disaffection from the regime as a necessary step to meaningful action to improve society, then one would draw the opposite conclusion from a rise in the "alienation indicator." But by bracketing alienation as a "social problem," the authors choose to conceal their own political biases. They ignore the political content of the issue and pass off as a matter of consensus what is actually their own partisan point of view.

How has this curious adaptation of medical and quasi-medical language to politics come about? The currency of the term "social problems" and of some of the language associated with it stem partly from the influence of the Chicago School in sociology. These writers published numerous studies of crime, prostitution, and other forms of "social pathology" during the early part of this century. But a still more important influence, I believe, has been psychoanalysis. For one of the major effects of the psychoanalytic movement has been to extend medical thinking and clinical language to the realm of social behavior. One result has been a change in the treatment received by those now designated as "mentally ill" and, perhaps as importantly, in the legitimations put forward to justify this treatment.

For bracketing persons as "sick" rather than as perverse, evil, or merely bizarre creates a license, and perhaps even an imperative, for some form of treatment. And, at worst, such treatment may be nothing more than coercion, backed by implied clinical sanction, to desist in behaviors which others find uncongenial or threatening. Often, of course, the recipients of such "treatment" have no desire to be "cured." Courts sometimes refer homosexuals for psychotherapy, for example, in lieu of overt punishment; yet organizations representing the homosexual community increasingly protest the definition of homosexuality as an illness. When the notion of pathology is used this way, the extension of medical reasoning to "disorders" of personality and social behavior becomes simply a new justification for the old business of stamping out threatening or dangerous thoughts and doctrines.

The underlying error in this application of medical language to social and political conflicts stems from the fact that somatic medicine enjoys a clearer view of its ultimate ends than does the study of "social problems." The preservation of life and the alleviation of suffering represent relatively easy values to agree upon. Serious disputes there may be over the value of this or that form of treatment, but these are debates over technique, over the most efficacious means to agreed-upon ends.

But such moral clarity is not granted us elsewhere, and certainly not in political life. If there is disagreement about what constitutes "healthy" personality development, there is incomparably more over the nature of "social health," to use the term employed in *Toward a Social Report*. And, in the absence of agreement on the nature of the ultimate "good society," it is hardly surprising that people cannot agree as to what constitutes symptomatology; the case of alienation illustrates the point.

The question of what social and political developments should hearten or disturb us turns, after all, on that contentious point of what forms of social action and social change are most likely to bring about a "better" society—obviously a highly partisan matter. Again, social conditions like crime, poverty, civil strife, and alienation do seem inherently undesirable; they may *appear* to bear the same relationship to social "health" that disease does to physical well-being. But while few would find these conditions desirable in themselves, reasonable people will disagree over what they portend for the overall life of society. Conditions which some might interpret as symptoms of disease, others would see as the first pangs of childbirth.

By designating disagreeable social conditions as "social problems," then, the experts would have us believe that such conditions are equally deplored by all, like disease or injury. This view would imply that the explanation for the existence of such conditions lies not in the workings of particular political forces but through some irrational "dysfunction" in the political system. Such an interpretation obviously suggests resolution through technical expertise rather than political action.

And yet, a close and critical look at the array of "social problems" in America today shows that few of them represent authentic "problems" in the sense of conditions equally undesirable from all political and social standpoints. Quite the opposite: conditions like pollution, racism, poverty, and the like are basically oppositions of interest—not social problems but social conflicts, overt or concealed. The situations giving rise to these oppositions would cease to exist if their presence did not benefit the interests of certain groups in society at the expense of others. To be sure, none of these conditions is desirable in its own right, but they nevertheless flourish because their continuation is, on balance, beneficial to some. The industrialist, for example, will not find pollution *ipso facto* desirable. But he will certainly prefer the continuation of pollution to the curtailment of his profits.

THE POLITICAL CONTENT OF EXPERT "SOLUTIONS"

Yet, if the assumptions implied in the "social problem" rhetoric are specious, it is easy to see why they are also immensely attractive. For by concealing the conflicts of interest which give rise to "social problems," the rhetoric makes it possible to avoid accountability for one's positions. A conflict, after all, inescapably requires one to take a stand. A "problem," on the other hand, is something everyone can safely oppose. Thus, no one is surprised to find organizations representing the medical profession establishing bodies for combating the "problematic" high costs of medical care. Such an action conveys the desired impression that physicians are as concerned about the high costs of medical care as anyone else. But while physicians supposedly do not find medical indigence a desirable state of affairs in itself, the fact remains that the astronomical charges paid by patients stand in direct proportion to the prosperity of those who collect them. One would stretch a point to claim that the "social problem" of high medical costs is equally and identically deplored by patients and physicians alike.

Similarly, government bodies sponsor countless studies and "action projects" aimed at the "solution" of the "poverty problem," the "racial problem," and the like. No doubt the planners hope that the public will interpret these gestures as signifying unanimous opposition within the government to these evils. But it does not take much reflection to see that conditions like racism or poverty thrive through the influence of groups which benefit from their perpetuation—and that these are groups on which the government depends for its existence. Institutional patterns of racism would disappear if many Americans did not systematically seek the continued subjugation of blacks. Poverty would pass away if those who have money did not prefer keeping it to sharing it with the poor. It is bizarre to find oneself insisting on points so obvious. But reading public pronouncements on these matters is enough to convince one that these conditions result from some disembodied malfunction in the mechanisms of society rather than from predominance of concrete political interests. If those in power were really wholeheartedly eager to change these conditions, it is safe to say that the increase in tangible "solutions" would be in direct relation to the decrease in rhetoric.

Thus, it should be clear why the participation of social scientists and other experts in problem-solving efforts entails a political advantage for those who hold power. For if questions of opposition of interest are officially ignored, the only debates left are discussions over technique, over the best means available for the attainment of mutually agreed-on ends. And since social scientists are seen, with some justice, as preeminent experts on the workings of society, who could be better qualified to hammer out the optimal solutions to vexing social problems? The visible presence of such experts, hard at work in their problem-solving efforts, is bound to enhance the credibility of the notion that everything possible is being done to set the situation right.

Now, none of this is to imply that the efforts of the professional problem solvers are inconsiderable or that the "solutions" which they propound are inconsequential. What passes for "solving" a "social problem" is often a delicate and demanding task of accommodating conflicting interests with a minimum of politically explosive protest from any side. It is often a matter of doing *something,* or of *seeming* to do something, to alleviate an offending condition, without actually striking at the powerful interests which benefit from it. In the case of pollution, for example, "solutions" tend to involve finding ways of making the reduction of pollution palatable and profitable to the industrial interests which do the polluting. Or, with racial conflicts, we get meticulously thought-out solutions like black capitalism, which would ostensibly add a measure of well-being to the situation of the blacks without actually disturbing the domination of the whites. Thus, the claim of the professional problem solvers to making a special contribution to public policy is often no hollow one. Anyone capable of persuading people that "solutions" to "social problems" are in the works, while not actually disturbing those who profit from them, can justly lay claim to expertise.

Nor is there anything *inherently* wrong with the application of expert skills to the execution of government policy. Political objectives, once set, never accomplish themselves; the need for application of the best available techniques in order to realize political objectives is universal. Those with expert skills who support the stated political ends of any government, and who believe such ends to be stated in good faith, may well want to contribute to policies to achieve those ends. This is as it should be. What is pernicious, however, is the notion that technical expertise can somehow obviate or circumvent the political issues inherent in supporting any government policy, can somehow forestall the problem of taking sides in the social conflicts that go by the name of social problems.

Nevertheless, this position is not only implied in the official pronouncements of the professional problem solvers but also explicitly and self-consciously developed by their spokesmen. These ideas have gone under the name of "pragmatism" or "instrumentalism" and have corresponded with the much-noted "end of ideology." The precise meanings of all these terms, let it be said, is subject to dispute. But all involve the notion that those who formulate policy should forswear commitment to any political philosophy or partisan program and concentrate, instead, on arriving at concrete solutions to specific social problems. By these lights, the criterion for evaluating any particular policy is its effectiveness in such problem solving, its ability to "get results," rather than its correspondence to any programmatic "liberal" or "conservative" model.

WHO INTERPRETS "THE PUBLIC INTEREST"?

One important vehicle for this position has been *The Public Interest,* the journal founded in 1965 by Daniel Bell and Irving Kristol. Bell, professor of sociology at Harvard, is author of *The End of Ideology.* He was also co-chairman of the Health, Education, and Welfare Panel on Social Indicators, whose consultations with the authors of *Toward a Social Report* led to the publication of that document. In their editorial statement in the first edition of *The Public Interest,* Bell and Kristol provided a manifesto for the "pragmatic," problem-solving approach to public policy. It is worth quoting in detail:

> . . . [Our] emphasis is not easily reconcilable with a prior commitment to an ideology, whether it be liberal, conservative, or radical. For it is the nature of ideology to *preconceive*

reality; and it is exactly such preconceptions that are the worst
hindrances to knowing-what-one-is-talking-about. It goes without saying that human thought and action is impossible without *some kinds* of preconceptions—philosophical, religious,
moral, or whatever—since it is these that establish the purposes
of all thought and action. But it is the essential peculiarity of
ideologies that they do not simply prescribe ends but also in-
sistently propose prefabricated interpretations of existing social realities—interpretations that bitterly resist all sensible
revision. *The Public Interest* will be animated by a bias against
all such prefabrications.[5]

Since its inception, *The Public Interest* has stuck to its stated
principles. It has devoted itself to studies on the use of social science expertise in public policy making, contributed generally by
professionals in the social science disciplines, and often by those
with close connections with the government. It has shunned discussion of political philosophy and eschewed open identification
of itself with any particular political position.

Nevertheless, the position of Bell, Kristol, and the other problem solvers has hardly enjoyed unanimous acclaim. Bell's prophecies in 1960 on the future of ideology were not fulfilled, and the
most acrimonious debates have since sprung up between the "pragmatists" and their more openly partisan counterparts. Noam
Chomsky, for example, identified the "pragmatic" cooperation
between academics and power holders as a key evil in his critique
of American policy. The "pragmatists" have not been slow to respond. Bell, for one, took special exception to the characterization
of his position in a review of Chomsky's book, *American Power
and the New Mandarins,* in the *New York Times Book Review.* In
a letter to that publication, he first quotes from the review:

> The "end of ideology" thesis thus provides a justification for
> precisely that "instrumentalism," that reliance on "experts,"
> which it purports simply to describe.[6]

[5] Number 1, Fall, 1965, pp. 3–4.
[6] May 11, 1969, p. 38.

Then he continues:

> And "instrumentalism" is described as "the concentration on
> the adequacy of means rather than the moral quality of the
> ends being sought."
>
> As the author of a book entitled "The End of Ideology,"
> let me say, flatly, that this is a complete caricature of my own
> views—in fact, a distortion of everything I have believed and
> written.
>
> In a half dozen essays in recent years on the role of techni-
> cal decision making, I have consistently argued that such tech-
> niques . . . can only clarify means, and never ends, and, at
> best, they can widen the choices so as to permit a more ra-
> tional examination of ends, which always remain moral
> choices.[7]

Obviously, strong feelings turn on the construction of the idea of
"instrumentalism." Nor is this exchange the only reason for drawing this conclusion. The charges traded back and forth between the
"pragmatists" and their critics were a bitter measure of the charged
intellectual and political atmosphere of the late 1960's and early
1970's, and these exchanges have continued to the present.

Certainly, neither Bell nor any other representative of the problem solvers has proclaimed himself in favor of the application of
expert skills without regard for the ends to which they are applied.
No one, in this post-Auschwitz era, is apt to take such a position.
Yet Bell and Kristol, clearly enough, have their work cut out for
them if they are to defend the position which they do take—the
position that it is possible to devise "solutions" to "social problems" without recourse to "ideology," without any particular political program, "whether it be liberal, conservative, or radical." This
is precisely the difficulty with social problem solving; it is a profoundly *political* enterprise from beginning to end, and its ideology is nonetheless important for being concealed.

Bell and Kristol clearly mean to give the term "ideology" a

---

[7] Ibid.

pejorative connotation, as though to indicate something fruitlessly doctrinaire or sordidly partisan. Beyond that, however, their implicit concept of ideology seems to be a series of guiding assumptions, setting out what states of the world are worth striving for and what forms of political action are most promising toward those ends. But even by this minimal definition of "ideology," any social problem solver, or any other policy advisor, must necessarily make "ideological" choices. Even the definition of social problems implies a choice among political philosophies, as the case of alienation shows. Indeed, every political group defines "problems" by its own partisan lights. To the conservative, social unrest will appear as the critical "problem" of the day, while to the radical the "problem" will appear as the machinations of those who hold power. Nothing can be defined as "problematic" without some model of what the social world should be, without some prescriptions of what forms of political action, or inaction, are appropriate to better that world. Whether these are called "ideological choices" or something else, they cannot be avoided in any political decision making, and certainly not in the "solution" of "social problems."

And if the definition of "social problems" involves choices which must be seen as ideological or political or partisan, so too, *a fortiori,* does the "solution" of such "problems." For the active or threatened opposition of interests which underlie the "social problems" means that any solution to such problems requires a choice as to which interests to favor. What, after all, could be more partisan or ideological than deciding which side to support in the major social conflicts of the day? In the case of the poverty "problem," it is safe to say that no officially entertained solution will involve, for example, confiscation of all private assets in excess of $100,000. The objections are hardly technical, since such a step would provide ample resources for redistribution. Rather, such a program would be "unworkable" on political grounds, because it would strike at the very groups on whom the government depends for its existence. Officially proposed solutions, as I have noted, thus tend to concentrate on ways of doing *something,* or *appearing* to do something, for the poor without really hurting the prosperous. The social problem solvers may win admiration for the political footwork necessary to arrive at such "solutions." But the choice involved in working within these constraints ought to be recognized for what it is—an act of political partisanship, a clear-cut renunciation of more sweeping steps toward the elimination of poverty.

Let me repeat, in conclusion, that none of this represents condemnation of the application of expert skills to official policy, on the part of social scientists or anyone else, as *ipso facto* evil. Anyone who wants to support the interests and purposes of those in power will be glad to participate in the formulation and execution of policy, and to bring to his or her participation any special skills available. In this context, social scientists should be especially adept at determining how various circumstances interact to produce an offending social condition, and, as Bell and Kristol would be the first to emphasize, at making certain that a given policy is realistically designed to bring about change. Further, as social scientists love to reiterate, their own usefulness as policy makers should increase with the continued development of knowledge in their various fields.

But cooperation in the exercise of power always commits one to share responsibility for the users of such power, in the broadest sense. There is nothing apolitical or anti-ideological in the use of technical skills for political purposes. On the contrary, the user cannot escape identification with the political positions of those who actually hold the power. The language of "social problem solving" may, unfortunately, lead people to believe that the politics have somehow been taken out of policy, as though there were a single "best interest" equally desirable to all groups in society. This vision is not only specious but also dangerous. It is dangerous because of the prospect that a government desperate to cool off brewing social conflicts and a community of professionals hungry for recognition may find it an irresistible vehicle. The result would be the imposition of highly partisan "solutions" in non-political guise. Certainly, we need expert technical advice to bring about any political program that we truly believe in. But the technical questions are easy, in present-day America, compared to the political ones.

2

Models of Relevance:
The Social Effects of Sociology

"You shall know the truth," the Scriptures tell us, "and the truth shall make you free." Some version of this doctrine seems to sustain most systematic social inquiry. True, not all students of society would necessarily regard freedom as the most important ultimate aim of their activities. Many would give first importance in this regard to the alleviation of human suffering, or the resolution of grave social conflicts, or the promotion of enlightened official policies. But nearly all would want to argue that their work has some usefulness which goes beyond their own satisfaction in carrying it out. These notions of how social inquiry can and should redound to some benefit for society as a whole are not just vague intimations; they potentially represent sociological models in their own right.

This study deals with such models, which I term *models of relevance*. I hold that these models play an extremely influential role in shaping sociological work—not only in applied sociology but also in purely academic studies.[1] Some sociological writings read as though addressed to potential activists or an aroused public, while others seem intended for a policy-making elite. Often, the former crackle with ringing judgments and moral indignation, while the latter tend more toward technical understatement and emotional reserve. These differences show the impact of differing models of relevance, as they guide sociologists' expectations of the long-term effects of their work. Other manifestations of such models include not only the style of organization and presentation of social inquiry but also, and perhaps even more importantly, selection of research problems and strategies. But though the influence of these models may be profound, sociologists have rarely subjected them to critical examination.

In this chapter, I aim to identify and analyze several models of relevance which have played an influential role in American sociology. I mean to take such models seriously as interrelated hypotheses in their own right about the workings of social systems. For models of relevance must deal with such issues as the relations between beliefs and action; the conditions of stability and change in social systems; the interactions between abstract ideas and material interest; and the role of power relations in shaping patterns of social change. All of these are eminently sociological questions. It would be surprising if the assumptions embodied in sociologists' models of relevance did not fit with their thinking on other matters.

Superficial consideration of these issues has often led to gross underestimation of their complexity. For from a *strictly technical* perspective, the usefulness of social insight is easily established. Any manager aiming to raise his firm's production will profit from the greatest possible understanding of the firm and its employees.

[1] For convenience, I am couching this argument in terms of sociology. Actually, I believe that many of the same points would apply, *mutatis mutandis*, for other social science disciplines.

Any would-be revolutionary, by the same token, will profit from the most thorough understanding of the institutions to be subverted. In calculations like these, social science insight facilitates social manipulation, just as natural science makes possible the work of the engineer.

This realization has led some thinkers to regard social science insight as a sort of universal solvent for the stickiest social problems. George Lundberg epitomizes this simplistic view in his book *Can Science Save Us?* The answer to the question in the title, of course, was a ringing affirmative; he wrote,

> Why is it that we find ourselves with thousands of research laboratories devoted to the application of the scientific method to physical problems, and almost none, comparatively speaking, devoted to research in human relations? Is it because human relations are functioning so smoothly that they need no attention? A glance at industry, our minority problems, and the international situation should be sufficient answer. Is it because, while physical research pays a tangible dividend in profits, improvement in human relations does not? Ask any employer what labor troubles, strikes, lockouts, slowdowns, and loafing is costing him, and in the end, costing all of us. Then why don't we risk a few million dollars in scientific research on human relations the way we risk hundreds of millions on industrial research. . . ?[2]

The superficiality of Lundberg's assumptions is only too apparent. Lundberg simply ignores the issues raised in the preceding chapter. Conditions which he wishes to see improved, like most situations which sociologists and others might regard as "ripe for improvement," entail conflicts of interest. "Labor troubles, strikes, lockouts, slowdowns and loafing" are troublesome precisely because they entail incompatible attempts to gain advantage. It may be easy to imagine how added insight might help either one contestant or another in these situations. But it is much more problem-

[2] (New York: Longmans, Green and Co., 1947), pp. 64–65.

atic to develop a formula for "rational solutions" to these difficulties which all concerned would acknowledge as such.

More generally, it is nearly always easier to assess the social effects of specific items of insight in specific situations than it is to judge the effects of whole categories of inquiry upon wide areas of social life. An industrial sociologist may determine, for example, that working conditions in a particular plant lead to greatly increased mortality among its workers. Disclosure of the finding may be certain to provide advantage for workers or to place management on the defensive. And the sociologist may assess such an outcome as satisfactory or not, depending upon his or her values or interests. But much more complex sociological judgments are required to assess the long-term social effects of studying occupational safety or industrial relations *in general*.

Models of relevance demand precisely these kinds of assessments. Industrial relations specialists ordinarily do not *only* aspire to illuminate particular conditions in particular establishments; most probably also hope that their work will contribute, however modestly or indirectly, to "better" industrial relations, or perhaps even a better world. Students of poverty, by the same token, probably aspire not only to enlarge understanding of specific forces in the generation of poverty but also to help alleviate the sting of poverty in general. Even those who would justify the study of society as a worthy end in itself would probably wish to picture the effects of their inquiries as at least not downright destructive of social well-being. And justification of any such beliefs requires assumptions about the "products" of social inquiry, about the "consumption patterns" governing reception of such insight, and about the effects of insight on social action.

What especially complicates such assessments is the open character of sociological communication. Like other scholarly disciplines, sociology institutionalizes mutual cross-checking of research procedures and publication of results for the attention of all interested parties. This means that the scholar can control "production" of social insight but not necessarily its "consumption." This fact poses a fundamental problem for any model of relevance, since all such models must provide some account of the uses of social insight.

The following discussion deals with five models of relevance. The aim is to make these models explicit and to evaluate them as sociological hypotheses in their own right. To be sure, we are some way from being able to test such models against specific data. But it is by no means impossible to assess the internal consistency of the models, and to weigh their plausibility as assertions about the working of the social world. This will mean posing the following questions about each:

> 1. Does the model embody a coherent idea of what benefi-
> cial results for society at large it seeks to promote? Is this
> vision one which other students of society might share? (I do
> not mean to ask here whether the underlying notion of social
> good is philosophically sound, but simply whether it repre-
> sents a plausible and workable basis for consensus among re-
> searchers.)
> 2. What are the "relevant" intellectual products supposed
> to redound to such results? What *form* of sociological research,
> in other words, is to have the beneficial effects?
> 3. What category of social actors are seen as the "con-
> sumers" of the relevant insight? Whose behavior, in other
> words, is supposed to be shaped by the insight in question?
> 4. Is it reasonable to expect the actions inspired by such in-
> sight to take the desired form? Do these actions have a chance
> of being effective to their intended ends?

The five models treated below are distinguished first as ideal types. Then passages from the writings of influential sociologists are presented to illustrate the actual manifestations of such types, and the strengths and weaknesses which they entail. As with all ideal types, none of these five is embodied in pure form in any empirical case. Each writer departs from or embellishes the ideal type at some point in his writings. Careful and coherent exposition of any model of relevance is rare, and many statements discussed below are fragmentary assertions of principles which may not be followed faithfully in practice. Still, the examples given here should illustrate how models of relevance shape expectations of sociological inquiry and demonstrate the difficulties inherent in such expectations.

Nor do these five ideal types represent all the models of relevance which are either logically possible or empirically influential. These discussions confine themselves to models which follow the Weberian assumption that empirical analyses cannot themselves yield prescriptions of ultimate value. Thus, I do not deal here with the doctrines of the Frankfurt School, whose studies of social antagonisms aim at revising the values of the antagonists. Those models entail serious difficulties in their own right, I feel, but much different ones from those of the models discussed here. While the models discussed below are hardly exhaustive, however, they probably represent the most influential ones in the development of American sociology.

MODEL I: NO NET EFFECTS

Perhaps the simplest model of relevance is one which posits no net input at all of sociological insight to any greater social good. For anyone espousing such a model, the inherent rewards of enhanced understanding would be the only possible justification for the efforts of the sociologist. I suspect that this model is especially unlikely to find defenders in anything like its pure form, at least among working sociologists. A few social scientists, however, have espoused variants of the doctrine.

For obvious reasons, those who despair of the possibility of social betterment through social insight do not develop any very clear concept of what such betterment would entail. Writers in this vein do, however, provide various accounts of the social conditions which preclude such change. One line of argument to this effect is to view all important social outcomes as governed by forces too powerful to be influenced by human ideas. A good example of such an argument comes from William Graham Sumner:

> It is at any rate a tough old world. It has taken its trend and curvature and all its twists and tangles from a long course of formation. All its wry and crooked gnarls and knobs are therefore stiff and stubborn. If we puny men by our arts can do anything at all to straighten them, it will only be by modifying the tendencies of some of the forces at work, so that, after a sufficient time, their action may be changed a little and slowly the lines of movement may be modified. . . . In the meantime spontaneous forces will be at work, compared with which our efforts are like those of a man trying to deflect a river, and these forces will have changed the whole problem before our interferences have time to make themselves felt. . . . Everyone of us is a child of his age and cannot get out of it. He is in the stream and is swept along with it. All his sciences and philosophy come to him out of it. Therefore the tide will not be changed by us. It will swallow up both us and our experiments. It will absorb the efforts at change and take them into itself as new but trivial components, and the great movement of tradition and work will go on unchanged by our fads and schemes.[3]

Pareto and Spencer, among the other early sociologists, also sometimes took positions like Sumner's. Perhaps they, like he, found this argument an opportune way of emphasizing the importance of the causal forces which made up their newly designated subject matter.

Not many present-day social scientists argue that their efforts are indifferent in their overall effects on social well-being. One partial exception is Edward Banfield and James Q. Wilson, who propose a subtler argument in favor of this model in their well-known book *City Politics:*

[3] "The Absurd Effort to Make the World Over," A. G. Keller and M. R. Davie, eds., *Essays of William Graham Sumner* (New Haven: Yale University Press, 1934), I, 105.

The reason why knowledge about politics (whether in the form of general propositions or as practical wisdom) will not lead to better solutions of social problems is that the impediments to such solutions are a result of disagreement, not lack of knowledge. Knowing how disagreements arise, how the parties to them act vis à vis each other, and the rules and practices by which certain institutions mediate them is not likely to be of use either in preventing disagreements from arising or in bringing them to quicker or more satisfactory resolution. Thinking that a general increase in the level of knowledge about politics will promote better and faster solutions of social problems is something like thinking that a general increase in the skill of chess players will lead to shorter games or to a "solution of the problem of chess."[4]

Banfield and Wilson, then, arrive at their position by taking quite seriously the issue which Lundberg ignores in his statement from *Can Science Save Us?* Their recognition of the antagonistic social interests in the "consumption" of social science insight leads them to the conclusion that increase in such insight will be self-canceling in its effects on social well-being.

Unlike Sumner, Banfield and Wilson seem to believe that social science insight may in fact help people to pursue their own interests more effectively. But the interests so promoted must necessarily be, as they see it, opposed to other interests facilitated by the same sorts of insights. Yet probably they would not want to insist that every single insight provides precisely the same measure of advantage to every interested party—as though every fact useful for fueling insurgents' criticisms would serve just as well in the defense of entrenched interests. More likely, they mean that the balance of advantage to all concerned would somehow sum to zero over the longer run.

The remarks by Banfield and Wilson are tantalizingly brief, and they do not pursue at length the implications of their position. It

---

[4] (Cambridge, Mass.: Harvard University Press and The M.I.T. Press, 1963), p. 3.

is interesting to note the results for their model of relevance of changing just a few of the key assumptions. Assume that one category of social actors had a special capacity to profit from sociological insight. The implication would then be much different; it would then imply that enhanced understanding would lead, if only in the long run, to a net advantage to that group's interests. Or what if, instead of their zero-sum assumption, one posited that certain forms of social change were advantageous to all parties? Then it would be reasonable to assume that social inquiry might result in net social betterment by disclosing the possibilities for such change. As the following discussion will show, various other models of relevance take these possibilities as points of departure.

Again, probably no social scientist would espouse the present model in its pure form, either on the Banfield-Wilson grounds or on any other. For arguing that true understanding counsels skepticism in itself implies that understanding is beneficial. Skepticism, after all, promises to save us the wasted efforts which might result if we mistakenly believed that understanding could lead to active steps to betterment. A judicious limit on expectations represents a significant social benefit in its own right.

Actually, all three of these writers take this position. Banfield and Wilson write:

> . . . the spread of knowledge about politics may also reduce the amount of well-meant but often harmful interference by citizens in the workings of political institutions. A public which understands the nature and necessity of politics may perhaps be more willing than one that does not to allow politicians to do their work without obstruction. . . . And it may be more aware of the risks it runs of damaging, or perhaps even of destroying, a tolerable system by attempting reforms the full effects of which cannot be foreseen.[5]

In this view, the "consumers" of social science understanding would be a wiser general public, who would know better than to

[5] Ibid., pp. 3–4.

run the risk of making things worse by ineptly trying to improve them. These are sentiments characteristic of many a conservative theorist. Sumner takes virtually the same position:

> The truth is that the social order is fixed by laws of nature precisely analogous to those of the physical order. The most that man can do is by ignorance and self-conceit to mar the operation of social laws. The evils of society are to a great extent the result of the dogmatism and self-interest of statesmen, philosophers, and ecclesiastics who in past time have done just what the socialists now want to do. Instead of studying the natural laws of the social order, they assumed that they could organize society as they chose. . . . Let us not . . . delude ourselves with any impossible hopes.[6]

To summarize: The idea that social science insight has no over-all bearing on social well-being obviously represents one major logical possibility among models of relevance. It is not, however, an easy position to defend. To do so, one must contend that perceptions of the social world make little significant difference in human action bearing on social betterment. For social science inevitably has at least *some* role in changing such perceptions. Further, even where certain elements of this model are defended, the defenses tend to subvert themselves. For insight leading to the conclusion that no effective action to improve conditions is possible itself represents a form of benefit.

MODEL II: DIRECT AND POSITIVE EFFECTS

A second obvious possibility is to attribute to social science insight a direct and positive role in enhancing social well-being. Unlike the view suggested in the Banfield and Wilson quote, this approach does not picture all social interests as standing in zero-sum relation to one another. Unlike models discussed below, this

[6] "The Challenge of Facts," A. G. Keller, ed., *The Challenge of Facts and Other Essays* (New Haven: Yale University Press, 1914), p. 37.

one does not look to any one group of social actors to act as the main "consumers" of insight. Instead, this model posits areas of possible improvement in social relations where change would be to the interest of all. By showing how to realize these possibilities of a "better" social life for everyone, it is thought that social science may lead to ameliorative change.

In its many versions, this model has probably been the most influential of any in the development of American sociology. The earliest volumes of the *American Journal of Sociology*, for example, abound with expressions of faith in the role of sociology in pointing the way to a more rational social world. These rather touching expressions, however, do not spell out in any detail how these ameliorative changes are to come about. But such accounts have become somewhat more common in the present-day social problems literature. Probably the most sophisticated and fully elaborated of these is Robert Merton's detailed theoretical statement in his *Contemporary Social Problems*. Indeed, it is among the most complete and thoughtful defenses given for any model of relevance. It warrants examination here in detail.

One key question facing any model of relevance, it will be recalled, is whether it provides a conceptually clear and plausible notion of what "improvement" in social conditions would entail. In this case, the way in which this issue is resolved is essential to the viability of the entire model. Merton deals with social betterment in terms of "solutions" to "social problems"; his rationale is as follows:

> The first and basic ingredient of a social problem consists of a substantial discrepancy between widely shared social standards and actual conditions of social life. Such discrepancies vary in extent and in degree of importance assigned them so that social problems are regarded as differing in magnitude as well as kind.[7]

[7] "Social Problems and Sociological Theory," Robert K. Merton and Robert Nisbet, eds., *Contemporary Social Problems* (3rd ed.; New York: Harcourt Brace Jovanovich, Inc., 1971), p. 799.

This definition obviously entails all the difficulties of those doctrines loosely lumped under the category of "value-consensus" theories. Can one really assume that a single, unified set of values exists for any society, or indeed, any smaller social system? Are not disputes over what constitutes "shared social standards" at the very heart of the conflicts which often pass as "social problems"? Is there any ground for certainty that the definition of these shared social standards is more than a projection of the values and predilections of the sociologist-observer?

Merton seems to acknowledge the validity of these objections. He writes:

> We must . . . be prepared to find that the same social conditions and behaviors will be defined by some as a social problem and by others as an agreeable and fitting state of affairs. For the latter, indeed, the situation may begin to become a problem only when the presumed remedy is introduced by the former. What is loosely described as "socialized medicine," for example, was defined as a social remedy by Walter Reuther and many others in his constituency of the AFL-CIO just as it was defined as a social problem by the successive presidents of the AMA and many others in their constituency.[8]

Is the designation of social problems, then, completely arbitrary, nothing more than a whim of the one who defines? Merton thinks not; there are, he claims, at least a core of conditions which nearly everyone holds undesirable, no matter what his political identifications. No one, in other words, is really in favor of violent crime, epidemics, or poverty. In such cases, he holds, there is a consensual, and hence independent, criterion that these conditions represent subjects for improvement.

Merton's sensitivity to these issues is not misplaced. The notion of shared standards of evaluation of social conditions plays two crucial roles in his arguments. First, it provides a criterion for designating what form of social "improvement" his model aims at.

[8] Ibid., p. 804.

Second, it gives a rationale as to why better understanding should lead to action toward this desired state. For if people come to understand possibilities for new social arrangements which are really advantageous to all, it is only reasonable to expect that they will act, sooner or later, to realize those possibilities. Such reasoning is central to the many versions of this model.

But there are difficulties. Certainly it is true that there exist categories of social conditions, "social problems," which no one would regard as good things in themselves. But even there, the *significance* of the offending condition, and the details as to what would constitute its betterment, are matters of partisan difference. Probably no one really finds industrial strikes, to take Lundberg's example, a preferred mode of social activity; all concerned would be pleased to have them settled if the settlement could be on their terms. But what people agree is that they would prefer things to be different, not necessarily *how* they would like things to change.[9] These facts create problems for any model of relevance.

Acknowledging difficulties in his first position, and the importance of some independent criterion of the problematic status of social problems, Merton continues:

> The fact that the conflicting values and interests of differentiated groups in a complex society result in disparate conceptions of the principal problems of society would at first seem to dissolve the concept of social problems in the acid of extreme relativism. But this is only apparently so. . . . For *social problems are not only subjective states of mind; they are also objective states of affairs.*[10]

[9] A number of writers, including some explicit critics of Merton, have recently rejected the notion of *any* strictly technical or purely objective definition of social problems. See Herbert Blumer, "Social Problems as Collective Behavior," *Social Problems* (Winter, 1971), Vol. XVIII, No. 3; Kitsuse and Spector, "Toward a Sociology of Social Problems: Social Conditions, Value Judgments and Social Problems," *Social Problems* (Spring, 1973), Vol. XX, No. 4; Ross and Staines, "The Politics of Analyzing Social Problems," *Social Problems* (Summer, 1972), Vol. XX, No. 1.

[10] Op. cit., pp. 805–806. Italics in original.

The "objective states of affairs" to which Merton refers are reckoned in terms of functional analysis. He argues that the inter-related elements of the social whole can be considered like those of a machine or an organism. In cases where a particular part fails to make its contribution in the fashion most propitious for the working of the whole, one attributes a dysfunction. Cases of multiple dysfunctions represent, on purely objective grounds, social problems. The role of the sociologist is to point out such objective failures of social systems, even when they are not publicly recognized or proclaimed as social problems.

But who defines the "proper" functions of any institution? Doesn't such a definition once again entail representing the standards of the observer as objective sociological reality? Merton denies this:

> When we say that a particular group or organization or community or society is disorganized in some degree, we mean that the structure of statuses and roles is not as effectively organized as it, then and there, might be. This type of statement, then, amounts to *a technical judgment about the workings of a social system*. And each case requires the sociological judge to supply competent evidence that the actual organization of social life can, under attainable conditions, be technically improved to make for the more substantial realization of collective and individual purposes.[11]

It is, of course, essential for Merton to insist that such judgments are "technical"—that is, objective—since the alternative is to define them in terms of the personal preferences of the observer. But who judges the "collective purposes" of a particular social element? The issue is no clearer here than in the "commonly shared standards" argument. Is the purpose of a welfare institution to provide maximum services to the poor or to keep the latter in a position of regimented and well-disciplined subsistence? Is the purpose of a firm to provide jobs for its employees, to aggrandize the

---

[11] Ibid., p. 820. Italics in original.

power of its top management, or to generate profits for its stock-holders? Indeed, how does one assess "effective organization" for "collective and individual purposes" when the latter are at variance with one another? Are featherbedding rules in a railway, for example, dysfunctional (for the purposes of the management) or functional (for the purpose of the blue-collar staff)? Observers will certainly have their own strong feelings about these matters, but is there really any objective, "technical" standard to transcend such feelings?

But Merton has a defense:

> A social dysfunction refers to a *designated* set of consequences of a *designated* pattern of behavior, belief, or organization that interfere with a *designated* functional requirement of a *designated* social system. . . .
> . . . It must be noted . . . that the same social pattern can be dysfunctional for some parts of a social system and functional for other parts. . . .[12]

But if this formulation solves a conceptual problem, it at the same time reintroduces the problem of *objectivity*. For the injunction to look for designated consequences to designated social units once again introduces the very relativism which Merton deplores. *Which* consequences of *which* social conditions should be assessed in defining a social problem? Featherbedding, for example, may be dysfunctional for the management of a firm but functional and indeed vital for the union organization. Where, in this case, does the "social problem" lie?

Again, there should be no question of the importance of these matters in terms of the requirements of any model of relevance. Without some criterion for identifying "problematic" social conditions, the model lacks the coherent objective required of it. Lack of such a clear-cut goal of efforts at ameliorative change also casts into doubt the identity and role of "consumers" of social insight. For if people really disagree in principle as to what constitutes

[12] Ibid., pp. 839–840.

"problems," then we cannot expect added insight to result in a coherent and harmonious program of change. We cannot expect scholars to act consistently in identifying conditions for study or in choosing insights concerning such conditions which might represent spurs to ameliorative action.

As we have seen, Merton believes that exposure of conditions which are both generally deplored and objectively dysfunctional will lead to a movement of public feeling toward eliminating the offending conditions. But are not many designated social problems, including poverty, racial injustice, and the like, rediscovered periodically, without permanent steps toward their alleviation? Acknowledging the argument, Merton answers:

> Sociologists do not claim that knowledge of the consequences attendant on current social beliefs and practices will automatically lead people to abandon the beliefs and practices that frustrate their own basic values. Man-in-society is not as strictly rational a creature as all that. The sociological truth does not instantly make men free. It does not induce a sudden rupture with demonstrably dysfunctional arrangements in society. But by discovering consequences of accepted practices and by making these known, the sociologist engaged in the study of social problems provides a basis for substantial reappraisals of these practices in the long run, if not necessarily at once. . . .[13]

"The long run"; it has the ring of Marxist pronouncements on the ultimate effects of social class relations on the course of history. But even assuming a modicum of consensus in designating some social condition as undesirable in principle, can Merton really show that the force of opinion in these cases is bound to prevail over other forces in the situation? To do so would be to ignore the considerable vested interests which profit from the existence of those things designated as social problems. Whether the force of "commonly shared standards" or the disapproval of "dysfunc-

[13] Ibid., p. 807.

tional" elements can necessarily prevail over these seems problematic, at best.

Take poverty as an example. Surely the existence of a bottom stratum of poor people poses all sorts of attractive advantages to others in society. Herbert Gans, in a chapter entitled "The Positive Functions of Poverty and Inequality," cites some fifteen positive social benefits forthcoming from the existence of poverty, ranging from ensurance that "dirty" jobs will be done to the contribution of the poor, through their political apathy, to the stability of the American political process. Along the way, he writes:

> . . . the poor subsidize, directly and indirectly, many activities that benefit affluent people and institutions. For one thing, they have long supported both the consumption and the investment activities of the private economy by virtue of the low wages they receive. . . . Examples of this kind of subsidization abound . . . ; for example, poorly paid domestics subsidize the upper middle and upper classes, making life easier for their employers and freeing affluent women for a variety of professional, cultural, civic, or social activities. Conversely, because the rich do not have to subsidize the poor, they can divert a higher proportion of their income to savings and investment and thus fuel economic growth.[14]

Poverty and "social disorganization," then, although seen as quintessential social problems, are actually a boon to major interests in American society. One wonders whether any such "undesirable condition" could continue to exist, were this not the case.[15]

To summarize: Merton's arguments, though the most thorough

[14] *More Equality* (New York: Pantheon Books, 1973), pp. 106–107.

[15] Consider, for example, the case of poverty and unemployment, both of which represent classic "social problems." Economists generally concede that a drop in unemployment in the United States tends to raise the rate of inflation. Government planners thus have accepted substantial chronic unemployment, at levels higher than would be politically acceptable in other industrial countries, as a "necessary price" for the control of inflation. So, unemployment and the resulting poverty may represent "social problems," but they are not so problematic as the alternative, i.e., full employment.

defense of any model of relevance considered here, fail to answer all of the questions facing such models. The most serious difficulties stem from his inability to provide a coherent standard to designate what improvement of social conditions actually entails. Evidently conscious of the importance of the issue, Merton tries at length to develop an objective standard for the existence of "social problems," and thence, a purely technical role for the social scientist in solving them. I have argued that these efforts fail. The standards which he proposes, if tried, would misleadingly identify "problems" or "dysfunctions" of particular people or groups as those of the social whole.

This difficulty, in turn, sets off a chain reaction of other troubles with his model of relevance. It casts into doubt, for example, the nature of the insights which might lead to social change. For if observers disagree as to what constitutes a "social problem," they will hardly be able to agree as to what forms of insight cry out for change. And given such dissensus, it is unclear how any coherent program of action for change could arise from sociological inquiry. Different "consumers" of social insight would draw different, and perhaps conflicting, implications for action from the analyses of "problematic" conditions. In short, it is difficult to believe that Merton's formulations, if followed, would lead to a coherent pattern of movement toward what people would agree was enhanced social well-being. And while one cannot exclude the possibility that other arguments in favor of this model may succeed where this one fails, Merton's position appears to be the most sophisticated we have on the subject.

MODEL III: SPECIAL CONSTITUENCY—THE PROLETARIAT

The difficulties of Merton's argument should at least be instructive. They demonstrate how hard it is to develop a program of enlightenment which promises to serve directly the interests of all elements in society. Vested interests in keeping "problematic" conditions as they are, and contests over what constitute "problems" in the first place, threaten to plague any version of the previous model.

These difficulties have led many writers to seek an altogether different approach. Their solution is to accept as inevitable the conflicting interests in programs for social betterment, and hence, in the uses of social insight. Instead of attempting to develop a form of research which redounds immediately to the interests of all, they propose to generate forms of insight useful, at least initially, to just one category of social actors. These "special constituency" models, as I call them, are predicated on the assumption that this one category of "consumers" of social insight has the power to act effectively in the longer-run interest of all of society. No doubt the most famous proponent of such an approach is Karl Marx. His program of social inquiry was strictly oriented to the proletariat, the "consumers" who, he felt, could make best use of any insight in the long run.

Marx—like most students of society, but more openly and candidly than most—saw his work as designed to bring about a better world. He considered it his mission to extend the realm of rational understanding over the workings of the social world. At the same time, he explicitly identified himself as a partisan of a specific set of embattled interests. Evidently he felt no conflict between these two positions. He based his research on openly available sources and published his findings and conclusions for anyone to read. Yet he assumed that his labors would have their beneficial social effects through the actions of only one element of the social structure. No one ever appreciated more keenly that social "problems" stemmed from oppositions of interests among different elements of society; no one would have more quickly discounted the possibility of providing insight which would work for the immediate benefit of all groups. And yet, crucially, Marx felt that the social groupings favored by his inquiries in the short run would reap from them an advantage which would in the long run work to the best interests of mankind.

What form of social betterment does this model of relevance

aim at? The answer, in Marx's case, was a particularly rich one. In the very long view, Marx's vision of the good society was one of a world of bounty, free of the coercion of the capitalist state and the irrationalities of the capitalist economy. But the immediate goal, of course, was a revolutionary overthrow of the capitalist system which embodied these irrationalities. It would be difficult to underestimate the significance of this combination of assumptions for Marx's model of relevance. For it made it reasonable to assume that a better, more beautiful, less conflict-ridden world in the longer run required action to produce more partisanship and strife in the shorter run. As Marx put it in *The Communist Manifesto,*

> If the proletariat during its contest with the bourgeoisie is compelled, by the force of circumstances, to organize itself as a class, if, by means of a revolution, it makes itself the ruling class and, as such, sweeps away by force the old conditions of production, then it will, along with these conditions, have swept away the conditions for the existence of class antagonisms and of classes generally, and will thereby have abolished its own supremacy as a class.
>
> In place of the old bourgeois society, with its classes and class antagonisms, we shall have an association in which the free development of each is the condition for the free development of all.[16]

Marx believed, as we all know, that insight as to the true workings of capitalism could aid the proletariat to hasten the break with the old system. Such insights represented the essential intellectual "products" in his model of relevance. Marx felt that his critiques of the capitalist system served only the interests of the proletariat, that his ideas were incapable of being turned to the use of antagonistic social groups. True, members of other classes, including intellectuals, students, dispossessed capitalists, and others might identify themselves with the proletariat and thus become part of Marx's special constituency. But Marx held that the prole-

[16] Karl Marx and Friedrich Engels, *Basic Writings on Politics and Philosophy,* Lewis S. Feuer, ed. (Garden City, N.Y.: Anchor Books, 1959), p. 29.

tariat as a class represented the only historical force with the ability necessary to make significant changes. And only they could profit from insight into the ultimate defects of capitalism.

One implication of these views was the rejection of all moderate social reform measures, such as attacks on discrete "social problems." For Marx, the "problems" of capitalism were of a piece; reformist measures would tend to delay the death of the terminal patient instead of hastening the birth of a newer, better system. This conclusion, like those on the consumption of Marxist insight, obviously depends for its validity on Marx's historical prophecies on the future of capitalism.

Do Marx's statements provide a coherent view of the state of social betterment to which his model of relevance is attuned? Would others share this view? It would be difficult to fault the ultimate vision of a world without want or coercion. But the shorter-term element of Marx's scenario of social improvement—exacerbation of the conflicts of capitalism, leading to a sharp break with the political and economic system—are obviously much more controversial. Whether such a sharp break is essential to any meaningful improvement in social conditions continues to stand as a point of contention between Marxists and their more moderate colleagues in social science.

One reason for skepticism on this point is the failure of key Marxist prophecies on the future of capitalism. It is now a truism that advanced capitalist societies have become, contrary to Marx's expectation, less polarized rather than more so. The bulk of the populace in these societies is both better off materially and more effectively integrated into political life than was the case in Marx's time. These changes make it difficult to maintain that the only really significant improvement in capitalist societies can come about through their destruction. One may, of course, hold that destruction of capitalism is preferable to its perpetuation, but that is a different matter.

Second, it is far from clear that political action inspired by

Marxist precept has always contributed to social betterment or to the alleviation of human suffering. Surely even the most sympathetic Marxist observer of communist and socialist regimes would want to concede that Marxist doctrine, as interpreted by the leaders of these states, has at least sometimes led to very serious human costs. And it goes without saying that no one has as yet seen anything like a radical break with the irrationalities which Marx attributed to capitalism—political repression, economic scarcity, oppressive state bureaucracy—in any Marxist regime.

Finally, part of the inadequacy of Marx's model of relevance has to do with the patterns of consumption of insight which he posits. It is by no means clear that the industrial proletariat has represented the main "consumers" of Marxian insight and analysis. In fact, intellectuals, peasants, students, and other groups have often figured much more importantly than industrial workers in this connection. Nor can one reject the possibility that resourceful elite groups may be able to use Marxian insight to further their own decidedly non-revolutionary interests. The very proliferation of Marxist thinking—its currency, in differing versions, in so many different contexts—belies any certainty about its overall effects on social betterment.

It would be easy to mistake these reservations about Marx's model of relevance for an attack against Marxist analysis in general. That is definitely not my intent. One can accept all of these misgivings and still retain a belief in many of the key Marxist insights. What I criticize here is not so much the main sociological content of Marx's ideas as his finely tuned assumptions relating social analysis to improvement of social conditions. For these assumptions are so precise, and so closely related to one another, that change in any one is apt to leave in doubt Marx's assurance of the historical results of his own social analysis.

To summarize: Marx's model of relevance represents an ingenious attempt to address a special constituency with the unique ability to bring about a better, more rational world. A key element of

his model was the supposition that the proletariat, though so estranged from the capitalist system as to have no interest in its perpetuation, would ultimately grow to possess the power to overthrow
that system. The importance of this assumption left his model
vulnerable to vicissitudes in the historical role of the proletariat.
Thus, the much-noted failure of the Western working classes to
grow into a dominant political and social force greatly undermines
Marx's position here. Marxist insight has infinitely enriched the
sociological vision both of Marxists and others. But whether that
insight has made it possible to avoid irrationalities and suffering of
the sort which Marx sought to banish forever is something which
even Marxists must now doubt.

MODEL IV: SPECIAL CONSTITUENCY—THE UNCO-OPTED

Difficulties with the Marxist model of relevance, particularly
those arising from historical events since Marx's time, have not
been lost upon left-oriented thinkers. Even those sympathetic to
the working class may now not find this special constituency the
most promising "consumer" of insights for social innovation. Perhaps as a result, a genre of research has arisen which is informed
by a somewhat different, though closely related model. What distinguishes this model is its orientation to a category of "consumers" identified as those uncompromised by allegiance to or manipulation by entrenched power. Adherents to the various versions of
this model can clearly trace their intellectual lineage to Mannheim.
But Mannheim was much more explicit in identifying his special
constituency of unattached intellectuals than more recent exponents
of this model have been in identifying theirs.

It is this model which seems to have informed most of the critical sociological studies of American society since the 1960's. These
studies picture America as dominated by certain selfish established
interests, interests which most of the time succeed in squelching
protest and innovation from below. The rather diffuse grouping at

the bottom of the social heap—including possibly the working class, but also the poor, the deviant, racial minorities, and the alienated more generally—represent the special constituency of the various versions of this model. Members of these groups or their representatives, it is supposed, will respond to critical insights on the true workings of American society by coalescing their latent strength and seeking change. Such action, the model assumes, will represent overall betterment of social conditions.

No spokesman for this view seems to have given as detailed an account of it as that given by Merton for his model. One must thus piece together the underlying assumptions from briefer remarks made in passing. But the model seems more than merely implicit in statements like the following one by Gary Marx in the introduction of his *Muckraking Sociology:*

> . . . I wish to argue that an important and little acknowledged potential for change lies in the educative role it [social science] can play in raising public issues. Such data and analysis can give us a clearer picture of our world, stripped of protective verbiage and without the usual selective perceptions (and misperceptions). If this picture involves a striking contrast between values and practices, it can be politically useful to those seeking change . . . social science can help articulate the value claims and suffering of ignored and powerless groups. . . . The social researcher can of course also be instrumental to change by studying sources of resistance and how advocates of change can be mobilized, by designing and helping implement new programs and conceptions of society and by evaluating the consequences of innovations.[17]

The difference between the various versions of this model and the positions of Merton, on the one hand, or of Karl Marx, on the other, are nuanced and significant. Like Karl Marx's model, this one envisages the relevant intellectual products as consisting of critical insights as to the true, rather than the ostensible, workings of society. Like Merton, on the other hand, Gary Marx and other

[17] (New Brunswick, N.J.: Transaction Books, 1972), pp. 4–5.

writers in this genre stress the dramatization of discrepancies "between values and practices." But adherents to the present model lack the Marxist faith in the ultimate historical triumph of their special constituency, while they also lack Merton's theoretical assurance that the conditions which they find unacceptable will meet with universal disapproval.

This latter difference manifests itself in the self-portrayal by these writers not as purely technical, objective commentators, à la Merton, but rather as engaged activists who do not hesitate to commit themselves in favor of those groups and values which they favor. A good example comes from the statement of Jerome Skolnick and Elliott Currie, who define their position in self-conscious contrast to Merton's:

> Social scientists, then, study social problems from the vantage point of committed people striving to make sense of the society in which they find themselves. There is nothing wrong with that, but it should not be mislabeled "disinterested" inquiry.[18]

Statements like this point to an important difficulty in this model of relevance. By rejecting the Mertonian role of dispassionate interpreter of society's own standards, writers like Skolnick and Currie gain in dramaturgy but lose in the theoretical coherence of their model of relevance. The preceding statement suggests that the sociologist's values or interests may not be the same as those of the larger society, that they may be "partisan" sensitivities on behalf of embattled groups. But this assumption provides no assurance whatsoever that the sociologist's insights into the circumstances of oppressed groups will be sympathetically received by most people. The sociologist may illuminate the suffering caused, say, to homosexuals by the attitudes and practices of the "straight"

[18] *Crisis in American Institutions* (Boston: Little, Brown and Co., 1970), p. 13.

world, only to find that most straight people regard such oppression as no more than fitting. The researcher may, of course, resolve to tell the story just the same, to throw his or her lot with the oppressed, whether the world sympathizes or not. This possibility is always latent in the role of the engaged sociologist. But it fits badly into a model of relevance, which requires some account of how insight is likely to succeed in making things better.

Skolnick and Currie write,

> To speak of something as a "problem" is to bring it out of the realm of the inevitable or the tacitly accepted, take away its "sacred" character, and suggest that it need not be the way it is. To focus on institutions in this way is to open them to public scrutiny and to insist on the responsibility for change. More generally, such an approach holds those in positions of authority, power, and influence accountable for their actions.[19]

For Merton, such a position is consistent; it implies a view of the sociologist confronting the public at large with conditions which affront its own standards. If Skolnick and Currie were to give this interpretation to the statement above, their position would really be virtually indistinguishable from that of Merton. But though they are not explicit, I do not believe that this is their intent. I believe that they mean to invoke standards of judgment more partisan, more peculiar to their own special constituency. And if this is the case, then there is little ground for faith that their appeals will be successful. By addressing their insights to embattled groups at the bottom of the heap of social privilege, they may solve a moral problem of not wishing to identify with the standards of the establishment. But their intent to serve the weak then risks becoming unconvincing simply because of the weakness of those they would serve. They provide no rationale as to how the "consumers" of their insights will be able to act effectively on the insight they provide.

[19] Ibid., pp. 15–16.

This difficulty seems endemic in all versions of this model. Consider the statement of C. Wright Mills:

> It is, I think, the political task of the social scientist who accepts the ideals of freedom and reason, to address his work to each of the other three types of men I have classified in terms of power and knowledge.
>
> To those with power and with awareness of it, he imputes varying measures of responsibility for such structural consequences as he finds by his work to be decisively influenced by their decisions and their lack of decisions.
>
> To those whose actions have such consequences, but who do not seem to be aware of them, he directs whatever he has found out about those consequences. He attempts to educate and then, again, he imputes responsibility.
>
> To those who are regularly without such power and whose awareness is confined to their everyday milieux, he reveals by his work the meaning of structural trends and decisions for these milieux, the ways in which personal troubles are connected with public issues; in the course of these efforts, he states what he has found out concerning the actions of the more powerful. These are his major educational tasks, and they are his major public tasks when he speaks to any larger audience.[20]

The ambiguity in Mills's position is precisely the same as that faced by Skolnick and Currie. What are the standards of judgment to be applied to the conduct of the powerful? If they are the standards of everyone, then Mills's argument is fundamentally the same as Merton's, and subject to all of the same criticisms. If not, then we must ask what standards Mills means to invoke, and why anyone else, possibly even including his fellow radicals, should necessarily be expected to share them.

The difficulties are perhaps even more serious when it comes to the supposed effects of Mills's analysis in bringing about the results which he would like to see. Surely, much of the appeal of

[20] *The Sociological Imagination* (New York: Oxford University Press, 1959), pp. 185–186.

Mills's writing stems from the implication that, in performing his highly critical analyses, he is in effect doing intellectual battle against the social forces which he deplores. He flaunts this appeal when he writes:

> There is no necessity for working social scientists to allow the political meaning of their work to be shaped by the "accidents" of its setting, or its use to be determined by the purposes of other men. It is quite within their powers to discuss its meanings and decide upon its uses as matters of their own policy.[21]

Given his combative political stance, Mills really must take a position like this one. To do otherwise would be to suggest that the utility of his work must be abandoned to the very forces which Mills opposes.

And yet, within the framework of Mills's own analysis of American society—as embodied, for example, in *The Power Elite*—it is difficult to accept any grounds for such confidence in the effects of his insights. For one must finally ask to whom Mills is addressing his critical analyses. Not, one supposes, to those at the top levels of the power hierarchy, since they are presumably so implicated in the rotten order that they will not heed; nor, one imagines, to the middle levels, which Mills describes as a "drifting set of stalemated, balancing forces. . . ."[22] And still less, one supposes, to those at the bottom of the heap, who represent a ". . . politically fragmented . . . increasingly powerless . . . mass society."[23] But what audience is left? If *publics,* in Mills's sense, have really been extinguished by the growth of mass society, there is really little hope of a responsive audience anywhere. Karl Marx, after all, could always address his appeals to the proletariat, his "special constituency." No matter how downtrodden, their historical cir-

[21] Ibid., p. 177.
[22] *The Power Elite* (New York: Oxford University Press, 1956), p. 324.
[23] Ibid.

cumstances were bound to press the Marxist message into their consciousness sooner or later, and to provide them with the strength to act on that message. Nothing in Mills's analysis gives any assurance of such an acceptance.

Indeed, there is an even darker interpretation which can be put to Mills's work. If the dominant interests—the power elite—really do command the media of communication, as he claims, if they have as thoroughly co-opted the previously autonomous centers of opinion, then who is really most apt to profit from the results of any sociological insight? If Mills's analysis is true, those who command the means of communication and other key resources of American society will have the power to put any useful insight to work for their own ends. Thus, one can imagine the power elite using Mills's work for insight into how to further their domination and more completely to defuse the opposition. One would not want to insist on this interpretation, but it seems at least a more plausible scenario in light of Mills's analysis than one which Mills would prefer.

To summarize: Placing hopes for "consumption" of "relevant" social insights on a special constituency of unco-opted actors solves some problems but raises others. It forestalls the necessity of defending the complicated historical predictions which burden Karl Marx's model of relevance. It obviates the need to rest one's hopes for change on the sensibilities of the majority or upon established institutions—both of which may seem responsible for the unsatisfactory state of things in the present. But the result is the lack of any special rationale for how the unco-opted consumers of insight may be able to assert their interests effectively. Karl Marx could rely on the historical growth of proletarian power; Merton could put his faith in an appeal to the normative standards and interests of society as a whole. But this model has neither historical predictions nor appeal to a universal standard to guarantee its results. The account of why the insights addressed to this special constituency should necessarily prevail in action has yet to be written.

MODEL V: SPECIAL CONSTITUENCY—GOVERNMENT
OFFICIALDOM

A final model of relevance is that oriented to agencies of the state as "consumers" of sociological insight. One might view this model as the mirror image of the previous one. Instead of seeing those most disaffiliated from power and institutional connections as the most promising vehicle of enlightened understanding, this model identifies established power-holders as most likely to use social science insight in the interests of society as a whole.

No doubt this is one of the oldest models of relevance; it has had especially many variants. The 1960's brought a resurgence of interest in this view—precisely at the moment when other enthusiasts began to take special interest in the previous model. As one might expect, however, exponents of the two models have not generally been friendly to each other's programs. Consider, for example, the following statement from Daniel Patrick Moynihan:

> All in all, the prospect is for a still wider expansion of knowledge available to governments as to how people behave. This will be accompanied by further improvement of the now well-developed techniques of determining what they think. Public opinion polls are already a daily instrument of government decision-making. . . . The day when mile-long petitions and mass rallies were required to persuade a government that a popular demand existed that things be done differently is clearly drawing to a close. Indeed, the very existence of such petitions and rallies may in time become a sign that what is being demanded is *not yet* a popular demand.[24]

The message is clear: Those in power, aided by the proper social science techniques, can determine the needs of society more efficiently than ever. More important, they can be counted on to meet those needs without unauthorized dissidence from below.

This model at least avoids the implausibility of placing faith in

[24] "The Professionalization of Reform," *Public Interest* (Number 1, Fall, 1965), pp. 15–16.

the actions of special constituencies which are inherently weak. Unlike the proletariat or unaffiliated actors, the government represents a special constituency which ought to have the power to act on social science insight, if anyone can.[25]

On the other hand, one may well wonder about the *interest* of government bodies in social science insight. The modern state, after all, represents a complex and potentially contradictory bundle of potentials for action. Which of these potentials is social science insight most likely to serve? Are the most important state uses of social science insight likely to represent steps which would widely be regarded as in the interest of "society as a whole?" Or is the state more likely to mobilize such insight on behalf of partisan or exploitative interests? Obviously, these questions raise all the long-standing debates over the nature and function of the modern state.

Again, we have few self-conscious attempts to deal with the complexities of this model of relevance. But most variants of the model seem to deal with these questions by recourse to a modified version of a "social problems" approach like Merton's. Consider the words of the influential report on the public role of social science published by the National Science Foundation in 1969:

> The Commission believes that among the American people there are a number of widely shared national and community objectives, and that social scientists can contribute to their achievement. Interethnic and interracial conflict; alienation of much of America's youth from society; multiple problems of man living in urban settings; various pollutions of man's environment; crime; mental illness rates; problems of alcoholic and narcotic addiction; problems of the educational process in the nation's schools—these are among the most visible and publicized concerns. . . .

[25] However, some writers have taken the position that "social problems" are inherently so complex as to defy even the full application of state power. Moynihan himself has adopted a version of this position in his more recent writings. See, for example, *Coping* (New York: Random House, Inc., 1973), p. 278.

At present, the social sciences, like the humanities, are a relatively unused national resource. Much of America's effort to achieve its aims makes little attempt to use this fundamental resource. The Commission asserts its doubt that this country can successfully solve its challenging and diverse social problems unless it draws upon the increasing capabilities of the social science community.[26]

The closeness to Merton's position hardly requires emphasis. The NSF authors believe that the problems addressed by government action are everybody's problems, problems of the whole of society. These writers seem to differ from Merton only in focusing their hopes for enlightened action specifically on agencies of the state.[27]

And certainly, this position suffers from the difficulties of Merton's. For the assumption that the state stands fully and unambivalently committed to the eradication of offending social conditions is dubious at best. Conditions like those cited in the NSF statement—racial injustice, pollution, and alienation, for example—represent results of government action as much as they represent situations which the government is committed to eradicating. To be sure, no one would regard such conditions as desirable in their own right. But the alienation of youth, noted by the NSF writers, stemmed largely from the Vietnam War and other harsh government policies. Those at the centers of power no doubt regarded these results as undesirable side effects of the war, but nevertheless worth the political price. Environmental pollution is likewise deplorable in itself, but it may often prove more acceptable than the political costs of effective action against the polluters.

---

[26] *Knowledge Into Action: Improving the Nation's Use of the Social Sciences,* pp. 3–4.

[27] While Merton by no means rules out state agencies as consumers of insight into social problems, the implication of his statements seems to be that any and all elements of society may potentially be able to act on these insights.

To oversimplify only slightly: This model can be persuasive only on the assumption that state agencies stand ready to act "in the interest of society as a whole," but are prevented from doing so only by ignorance. Were this the case, the statements by Moynihan and the NSF writers would be justified. But as a blanket principle, such an affirmation implies an unacceptably optimistic statement of the government's willingness to do the "right" thing.

No doubt, there do exist policy areas where inadequate knowledge represents the main obstacle to effective state action in the general interest. Such situations might include combatting an epidemic or finding a way of preventing earthquakes. In cases like these, where social science insight or any other form of understanding has a purely technical role to play, it may assist in achievement of goals already specified. But most distressed social conditions, I have argued, are not like this. Instead, they represent cases where the government's political will for change is ambivalent at best. They are troublesome because they entail conflicts of interest among two or more parties; and those powerful interests responsible for the offending condition nearly always have a major say in government action. This creates real complications for any model of relevance stressing faith in government action as the vanguard of social amelioration.

Occasionally one comes across a statement in favor of a position which is so blatantly faulty as to dramatize the flaws in the underlying principle. A case in point here might be Professor Ithiel Pool's manifesto in favor of social science participation in the activities of the CIA:

> . . . there are a great many things that we have learned to understand better through psychology, sociology, systems analysis, political science. Such knowledge is important to the mandarins of the future for it is by knowledge that men of power are humanized and civilized. They need a way of perceiving the consequences of what they do if their actions are not to be brutal, stupid, bureaucratic, but rather intelligent and humane.

> The only hope for humane government in the future is through
> the extensive use of the social sciences by government.[28]

Then he continues, a few pages later:

> The CIA, as its name implies, should be the central social re-
> search organization to enable the federal government to under-
> stand the societies and cultures of the world. The fact that it
> uses as little social science as it does is deplorable. We should
> be demanding that they use us more. Do you feel that the U.S.
> government does not seem to understand Vietnamese villagers,
> or Dominican students, or Soviet writers? If you think that
> Washington could act better if it had a deeper comprehension
> of the social processes at work around the world, then you
> should be demanding that the CIA hire and write contracts
> with our best social scientists.[29]

The flaws in Pool's reasoning are so transparent as hardly to require comment. It is ridiculous to assert that social science or any
other form of insight can render "humane" the action of any
agency whose ends are not humane to begin with. The kind of
"understanding" conferred by social science is instrumental understanding, i.e., greater efficiency in the pursuit of existing goals. For
anyone who mistrusts the basic aims of the CIA or any other
agency, enhancing that agency's ability to act by granting it access
to social science skills would hardly promise to humanize its opera-
tions. Rather, it would render more effective the pursuit of what
may well be highly inhumane goals.

To summarize: Choice of government officialdom as "consumers" of social insight at least forestalls the embarrassments of designating constituencies too weak to act. But the established nature
of government power makes it difficult to argue that government
institutions, if only better informed, would necessarily act to improve social conditions. The burden lies upon proponents of this

[28] "The Necessity for Social Scientists Doing Research for Govern-
ments," Irving L. Horowitz, ed., *The Rise and Fall of Project Camelot*
(Cambridge, Mass.: The M.I.T. Press, 1967), pp. 267–268.
[29] Ibid., p. 271.

model to show how government agencies will choose specific forms of social insight as bases for specific policies. They must demonstrate how such information would enable the state to act decisively where it has not managed to do so thus far. This is no small task. Lacking answers to these questions, this model remains unacceptably equivocal.

CONCLUSION

The last ten years have seen a remarkable development, among American sociologists, of reflective concern with the workings of sociological inquiry. Some expressions of this concern have come in the form of semi-historical accounts of the unfolding of sociological thought. Perhaps the best-known examples in this genre are Gouldner's *The Coming Crisis of Western Sociology*[30] and Friedrichs's *A Sociology of Sociology*.[31] Other manifestations of the same concern have been quantitative studies of citations and other recognition of published work—for example, the work of Stephen Cole.[32] A major theme in all of these writings has been "paradigms," "domain assumptions," and other immanent principles in the organization of sociological inquiry.

Clearly, models of relevance represent yet another such principle, one with its own force in shaping sociological theory and research. The preceding discussion should demonstrate just how far-ranging the influence of these models is. Yet, the remarkable thing is how little developed most versions of these ideas are as coherent sociological accounts. All of the models examined above have proved to embody some very serious ambiguities or implausibilities.

These deficiencies, however, are instructive. In every case, the

[30] (New York: Basic Books, 1970).
[31] (New York: The Free Press, 1970).
[32] "Scientific Reward Systems: A Comparative Analysis," in Robert A. Jones, ed., *Research in the Sociology of Knowledge, Science and Art* (Greenwich, Conn.: Jai Press, forthcoming).

most serious difficulty seemed to arise in the attempt to take account of the conflicting interests which surround those social conditions deemed "ripe for improvement"—and hence, which bear upon the insight which might lead to such improvement. To oversimplify slightly: Accounts of how social arrangements could be "better" do not necessarily provide grounds for reshaping the concrete interests and prerogatives of those who oppose such change.

To be sure, different models run up against this conundrum in different ways. The brief statement from Banfield and Wilson, for example, viewed the oppositions of interests underlying social problems as an absolute obstacle to gains for society "as a whole." Merton and the exponents of state officialdom model, on the other hand, took exception to this severe view. They held that certain conditions were inimical not only to the interests of limited groups but to those of all members of society. Identification and understanding of these conditions could thus lead to action to improve them. But the conflictual setting of such "social problems" plagues these arguments in two ways. First, spokesmen for different social groupings and interests are bound to differ in their interpretation of what social conditions represent "problems." Second, even granted a measure of such agreement, it is difficult to see how the powerful interests profiting from "problematic" arrangements will necessarily be moved to accept change. Popular interest in ameliorative change may become a force in such situations, but these models give no reason to believe that such forces must necessarily predominate.

Special constituency models focusing on downtrodden groups—either the proletariat or disaffected groups in general—suffer from the obverse of these difficulties. These models, too, must show how the insights which they would foster would conduce to ameliorative change. These "special constituencies" at least share an interest in *some form* of change, though everyone knows that insurgents' programs for change may conflict with one another and even with themselves. Perhaps even more seriously, the very disenfranchisement of these special constituencies makes it difficult to believe that they will be able to act effectively on the implications of social insight. Arguments to how the weak will become strong—either through the historical growth of proletarian strength, as Karl Marx would have it, or through some other process—have not been wholly convincing.

For anyone who has entertained hopes that sociological inquiry will somehow speak to the needs of society as a whole, these ambiguities are unpleasant to confront. I suspect that most of us have entertained such hopes, at least at some point. And I know of virtually no attempt to assess these ambiguities and contradictions directly, without attempting to explain them away. The unique exception is Barrington Moore's recent work, *Reflections on the Causes of Human Misery,* subtitled *and upon Certain Proposals to Eliminate Them.* The ability to confront painful uncertainties without flinching is the outstanding feature of this book.

Moore's stance in the past has often been a radical one. These radical instincts are still evident here—for example, in his predilection for sweeping, social structural explanations of human misery as against the piecemeal "social problems" approach. But what is most remarkable about *Reflections* is the work's transcendence of many stale political debates in dealing with issues of universal concern. Often, for example, his statements are ones which Merton could accept without difficulty:

> . . . the main task becomes one of trying to assess the underlying currents of social change, their direction and power, *together with* the human costs of any effort to change their direction and that of refusing to make such an effort. . . .[33]

In other passages, Moore aligns himself more directly with the left, and his words sound as if uttered by C. Wright Mills.

> From this general assessment there follow certain obligations for the academic intellectual. The first is to try to uncover and expose the roots of violence and the threats to human freedom

[33] *Reflections on the Causes of Human Misery* (Boston: Beacon Press, 1972), p. 13.

that derive from the prevailing social order. Under present and foreseeable circumstances in the United States this conception of his obligation places the critical rationalist in sharp opposition to official liberalism as expressed by political leaders. . . *.[34]

Yet, elsewhere in the book, Moore goes more deeply into the assumptions involved in such statements, and confronts directly the difficulties which Mills and others ignore. Early in the book, for example, he explicitly rejects the idea that the social analyst can, as Mills would have it, remain in control of the social effects of his writings. Moore remarks,

> . . . one has to let the political chips fall where they will in serious social analysis. There is no innate guarantee that valid social analysis will always yield conclusions favorable to the humanitarian impulse.[35]

Then, most significantly, Moore adds in a footnote to this remark:

> I used to think that there might be some general drift in that direction because the dominant groups in any society are generally the ones who have more to hide about the way the society works. Hence critical exposure would generally favor the Left. Further investigation into the character of lower-class oppositional and revolutionary movements has made me more aware that they too have a great deal to hide (and to exaggerate) for their own political reasons. On that account I have become skeptical of any such drift.[36]

This is really a very telling observation. Here Moore rejects the notion that any model of relevance can provide assurance of the ameliorative effects of social inquiry. In honestly confronting this ambiguity, which Moore surely does not regard with equanimity, he parts company with Merton, Mills, and a wide variety of others.

Taken together, these quotes might suggest a confused or con-

[34] Ibid., p. 102.
[35] Ibid., p. 9.
[36] Ibid.

tradictory approach to the problem at hand. Such a reading, I think, would be excessively harsh. It would do greater justice to say that Moore confronts some agonizing issues facing any student of society and in so doing refuses to make closure where other writers would insist on doing so prematurely. He obviously believes that critical inquiry into the mechanisms of social life offers the best hope for alleviating human misery. Yet Moore has too much appreciation of the vagaries of history and ideas to hold out the promise that knowledge *must* inevitably lead to liberation. He is compelled to place his faith in reason, but too honest to portray such a commitment as more than an act of faith.

In their most fundamental form, the issues with which this study has been concerned are those of the ultimate causes of human suffering. Is ignorance the worst enemy of mankind, the source of most social ills, or is the enemy mankind itself? Will increased understanding of social life provide people with the tools necessary to control the social miseries which plague them? Or will such understanding simply sharpen the contests which pass as "social problems"? Will superior social analysis enable us better to perceive and to pursue those interests which we hold in common? Or will it enhance the destructive power of the contestants in those areas where interests are opposed? Surely anyone who pretends to certain knowledge on these points is deceiving either himself or his hearers.

Models of relevance will continue to have their influence on sociological practice. Appreciation that the social effects of sociology are less than certain should not deter people from embracing models of relevance as matters of faith, if not as received wisdom. But the bases of choice even among uncertain alternatives need not be wholly irrational. Careful analysis of competing models of relevance should at least help distinguish between more and less promising possibilities. Thus, we ought to entertain such questions as: How are the results of different programs of social investigation likely to serve major interests in society, in foreseeable social circumstances? How is the "consumption" of sociological insight likely to be shaped by its usefulness to various contestants in ongoing social conflicts? Are there limited areas in which sociological understanding might be useful to all or nearly all elements of society, and if so, what sorts of social insight would be most useful here? These questions may be extremely difficult, but they are at least empirical, sociological questions, ones which we ought to be able to attack, if anyone can. And they have not received the attention which they demand.

If I were more certain of any one model, perhaps I could close with an expression of confidence about the ultimate social benefit which might stem from these remarks. But perhaps it would be more appropriate to cite the epigram chosen by Barrington Moore for his book on the causes of human misery—from Joan Robinson's *Freedom and Necessity:* "Anyone who writes a book, however gloomy its message may be, is necessarily an optimist. If the pessimists really believed what they were saying there would be no point in saying it."[37]

[37] (New York: Pantheon Books, 1970), p. 124.

3

Social Science and the Clash of Political Philosophies

The preceding chapters have shown how persistently political choices thrust themselves into any formula for rational social inquiry. Every program for research and reflection on behalf of society "as a whole" appears, on close examination, loaded with special advantage for the partisans of particular political viewpoints. One response to this situation might be to turn the spotlight of social science analysis on political doctrine itself. Perhaps such examination may yield a way of distinguishing "good" or "reasonable" political positions from irrational or useless ones.

Or is it in the nature of political philosophies to yield answers to such questions at all? Widely divergent reactions assert themselves on this question—sometimes even within the same person. On the one hand, it seems no more than reasonable that social scientists should have something useful to add to political controversies, especially where the conflicts touch on areas of their special expertise. On the other hand, the quickest look at the history of such controversies suggests how. resistant they are to revision or change

through infusion of new information. Perhaps even more importantly, many see the key differences involved in the clash of political
philosophies as differences of value rather than differences of fact.
And the former, it is held, lie outside the scope of sociological discussion. Whether this represents a reasonable diagnosis is the question which this essay aims to address.

WEBER AND RUNCIMAN

It is, of course, mainly from Weber that modern sociology derives its sensitivity to the distinction between fact and evaluation.
The fundamentals of Weber's position are well known. The endless variety of social forms, in his view, corresponded to a multiplicity of culturally shared views of what is ultimately desirable in
social life. The analysis of such value positions, and particularly of
their role in social action, was among the key tasks of the sociologist. But sociological analysis could never provide grounds for
evaluating the values themselves.[1] Choice among ultimate values,
in other words, was metaphysical or arbitrary; analysis of empirical
fact, including sociological analysis, could never justify such a
choice. Thus, the sociologist *as a sociologist* had no grounds for
criticizing the value positions of those he studied, any more than
one could sociologically appraise the doctrine of original sin or a
liking for strawberries.

It is equally well known that Weber drew from this position
some strict, anti-prophetic conclusions on the role of the sociologist in political controversies. Any political position, he held,
rested on assumptions of ultimate value. This value content of political doctrines or philosophies placed any choice among them beyond the reach of sociological analysis.[2] Sociological analysis might
help to clarify the differences, say, between aristocratic conserva-

[1] H. H. Gerth and C. Wright Mills, eds., *From Max Weber: Essays in
Sociology* (New York: Oxford University Press, 1946), p. 143.
[2] Ibid.

tism and fascism by analyzing the social bases of their support, or by showing the implications of implementing their political programs. But such empirical analysis could not help to pass judgment on the *worth* of their positions, nor on that of any other political position. Choice among such doctrines, as an affirmation of ultimate values, could only be arbitrary. The sociologist's choices were thus attributable to his own value predilections; they did not represent sociological truth, to be expounded *ex cathedra*.[3]

It is significant that Durkheim, writing at about the same time, developed a position almost diametrically opposed to Weber's. Durkheim's view was that societies, viewed as functional wholes, had "needs" for specific social arrangements, needs which could be determined through sociological analysis. Such analysis could enable the sociologist to prescribe the "normal"—and hence, desirable—conditions for any society, even including the necessary forms of morality.[4] Thus, the sociologist by no means went beyond his competence in proscribing communism or unrestrained free enterprise as objectively inappropriate, say, for early twentieth century France. Durkheim, of course, took precisely such positions and advanced sociological arguments to justify them.[5]

I doubt that any modern sociologist would follow Durkheim quite as far as he went in this particular argument. Unqualified assertions that sociology can prescribe the "correct" moral and political arrangements for any particular society now have an arrogant ring. Nevertheless, modern functionalist doctrines often come close to this position. Merton's analysis of the functional interrelation of institutional elements, as the previous chapter showed, yields judgments of whether any particular practice or institution is making its "proper" contribution. And such judgments, in turn,

---

[3] Ibid., pp. 145–146.

[4] *The Rules of Sociological Method* (8th ed., New York: The Free Press, 1938), pp. 64–75.

[5] See Steven Lukes, *Emile Durkheim* (London: Allen Lane, The Penguin Press, 1972), esp. pp. 268–274.

enable the sociologist to identify some social arrangements as sound
and others as "problematic."[6] Likewise, in his writings on social
evolution, Talcott Parsons has no hesitation in designating some
social arrangements—for example, individualism and social strati-
fication—as progressive and others—such as socialism—as spokes
in the wheel of social progress.[7] The reasoning underlying both
these positions is directly derived from Durkheim's thinking.

In the previous chapters, I criticized the argument that sociological analysis can, on strictly objective or technical grounds,
specify the concomitants of "healthy" or "normal" social relations.
The purpose here is hardly to recapitulate those arguments, but
only to emphasize what a contrast they represent to Weber's position. Yet, much as I disagree with the functionalist position, I feel
that the extreme opposite, as embodied in Weber's skepticism, is
also unsatisfactory.

Present-day sociologists have not confronted this issue as directly as one might expect. One of the few thoughtful attempts to
criticize Weber's skepticism has come from the distinguished British sociologist W. G. Runciman. There is no need, Runciman argues, to accept the position that all political doctrines deserve to
be taken equally seriously by the sociologist. While conceding that
sociological analysis cannot in itself pass on the merits of such
positions, Runciman points out that certain value choices can be
shown inherently unsuitable as bases for social life:

> No political philosopher has ever suggested that suffering
> should be maximized, or that it is the duty of the State to take

[6] "Social Problems and Sociological Theory," Robert K. Merton and
Robert Nisbet, eds., *Contemporary Social Problems* (3rd ed.; New York:
Harcourt Brace Jovanovich, Inc., 1971), pp. 819–820.

[7] "Evolutionary Universals in Society," *American Sociological Review*
(April, 1964), Vol. XXIX, No. 2, pp. 339–357. John Goldthorpe has recently developed a penetrating critique of such arguments in his article
"Theories of Industrial Society: Reflections on the Recrudescence of Historicism and the Future of Futurology," *European Journal of Sociology*
(1971), Vol. XII, No. 2.

measures ensuring that contracts and promises are never kept. This does not mean that all political philosophies are simply different recommendations of the most efficient means to agreed ends. It does mean, however, that certain minimum ends are agreed upon, and that it is only beyond this point that we shall be confronted with disagreements where Weber's argument comes into its own.[8]

Or, as he notes elsewhere in the same essay, ". . . we need no more take seriously the political philosophy of . . . a suicide club than we did the flat-earthers' geography."[9]

Now, this observation is helpful as far as it goes, but it hardly serves to resolve the most serious problems posed by Weber's doctrine. The political questions which draw most of our attention most of the time, the questions of public policy and public opinion which we would most like to resolve, are hardly comparable to the flat-earthers' philosophy or the political doctrines of a suicide club. Instead, the major controversies are over contending programs, all of which are at least vaguely plausible, for action on current issues. Most social scientists will not lose much sleep over their inability to refute the value predispositions of a suicide club. But many would like to contribute to debates such as those over alternate positions on educational policy or public expenditure.

For the reconciliation of these more serious and much more important differences, Runciman offers little help. Indeed, he seems to accept that sociological analysis as such can do little to resolve basic antagonisms of contending political philosophies. If such resolutions are to occur, he argues, they are more likely to resemble "conversions" of religious or aesthetic persuasion than they are the settling of a debate over matters of fact. At best, he claims, one might encourage such conversions by what one might term "sympathetic exegesis" of one's own value position:

[8] *Social Science and Political Theory* (2nd ed.; Cambridge: Cambridge University Press, 1969), p. 170.
[9] Ibid., p. 169.

> One tries . . . to secure the approval of one's interlocutor to
> the picture of the ideal society conjured up by the implementa-
> tion of one's own political philosophy, and one tries to get
> him to accept that terms of approbation are more appropriate to
> one's own picture than to his. "But surely," one says, "it is
> more important that nobody willing to work should be allowed
> to remain unemployed than that extra entrepreneurial initia-
> tive should be rewarded by incentive payments," or whatever it
> may be.[10]

No doubt, these sorts of suasions do sometimes bring about the
conversion experiences which Runciman has in mind. But one
would hardly want to put faith in this method as a general program for resolving clashes of political world views. For the strategy which Runciman describes is really not much different from
our usual response in attempting to make our political positions
attractive to others. And everyone knows that such attempts are not
always successful.

In fact, by proposing this method, Runciman implicitly accepts
what I would consider the fundamentals of Weber's skeptical position—the notion that sociological analysis itself cannot help to
pass on the substance of differences among political doctrines. By
suggesting that any choice among such doctrinal positions must be
in the nature of a conversion, Runciman implies that such differences are primarily questions of predilection, not disputes which
can be clarified through analysis of facts. Thus, we are left with
the restricting conclusion that sociology may analyze political doctrines but cannot help to decide among them.

An intellectual stalemate of this kind is often a signal that the
wrong questions are being asked. I believe that this is the case
here. Let us concede that sociological analysis—that is, the examination of facts and empirical evidence—cannot, by definition, resolve the strictly *metaphysical* questions involved in the assessment
of global political doctrines or philosophies. It remains to inquire

[10] Ibid., p. 172.

whether the arguments generated by the clash of such world views stand or fall only in terms of such assertions of ultimate value.

THE EMPIRICAL CONTENT OF POLITICAL DOCTRINES

What we mean by a political doctrine or philosophy—such as aristocratic conservatism, nineteenth century liberalism, or anarchism—is not simply a set of value affirmations. When we speak of such positions, we mean to suggest both sets of ideas concerning what is ultimately good in social life *and* a series of *empirical propositions* on how societies work. These propositions may be diffuse and general, applying to an enormous variety of situations, but they do open the way to some sort of empirical evaluation of the doctrine. "Compare the *results* of implementing my doctrines with those of implementing alternative views," almost any political argument implicitly goes, "and you will see that the former are preferable to the latter—even by your own value standards." To be sure, it is often extraordinarily difficult to determine exactly how the implementation of broad political doctrines would work, and what the effects of such implementation would be. But the appeal involved is certainly empirical, at least in principle. Such statements are far from being arbitrary expressions of preference, like taste in art or food. They are not appeals to *ultimate value* in the sense discussed by Weber; they are affirmations of the *instrumental value* of broad policies or practices.[11]

If this observation is correct, it should not be hard to document. Consider, as an example, one of the scriptural sources of conservative thought, Edmund Burke's *Reflections on the Revolution in*

[11] See, for example, Austin Ranney, "The Study of Policy Content," Austin Ranney, ed., *Political Science and Public Policy* (Chicago: Markham Publishing Co., 1968), p. 16. Ranney writes ". . . many, maybe most, value statements are instrumental rather than ultimate. . . . And any statement about the instrumental value of something has a major empirical component appropriate for the hypothesis-testing techniques of the empirical political scientist."

France. Reading through this work, one encounters many statements which stand as pure outpourings of political emotion—value affirmations in their unalloyed form:

> France, by the perfidy of her leaders, has utterly disgraced the tone of lenient council in the cabinets of princes, and disarmed it of its most potent topics. She has sanctified the dark, suspicious maxims of tyrannous distrust, and taught kings to tremble at . . . the delusive plausibilities of moral politicians.[12]

If these sorts of assertions were the only ones found in Burke's writing, we would be justified in regarding them as beyond the pale of sociological analysis. The "perfidy" of the revolutionary leadership and the "lenient" quality of the *ancien régime* are simple expressions of Burke's moral evaluations.

But these expressive outpourings accompany arguments which, though identical in tone, are clearly empirical in reference. Still speaking of the revolutionary leadership, Burke continues:

> They have found their punishment in their success. Laws overturned; tribunals subverted; industry without vigor; commerce expiring; the revenue unpaid, yet the people impoverished; a church pillaged, and a state not relieved; civil and military anarchy made the constitution of the kingdom; everything human and divine sacrificed to the idol of public credit, and national bankruptcy the consequence. . . .[13]

The last word, *consequence,* is the key. Adumbrating conservative arguments on a wide range of issues, Burke holds that rapid and discontinuous breaks with established, traditional authority lead to *bad results.* And the badness of the consequences, he implies, should be evident even to those who do not initially share his conservative values.

Burke's *Reflections,* of course, take the events in France as their theme. But the empirical content of political doctrines is equally evident if they are considered in their most abstract, least

[12] (Garden City, New York: Anchor Books, 1963), p. 442.
[13] Ibid., p. 443.

"applied" form. Consider, for example, the doctrine of nineteenth century liberalism—that is, the laissez-faire philosophy which passes for conservatism in America. Those who embrace this doctrine no doubt do often espouse certain characteristic ultimate values—for example, the notion that self-reliance represents one of the highest moral qualities. But when one thinks of this position, one thinks not only of value assertions but also of a host of more-or-less empirical ideas. The laissez-faire proponent, for example, is apt to hold that policies inspired by his position generate higher rates of economic growth than do alterative strategies. Such results, it will be held, are likely to lead to greater prosperity for all, if only in the long run. Similarly, the argument of classical liberalism against subsidies to the unemployed is not merely that such measures are in themselves morally objectionable. Instead, the free-enterprise spokesman holds that such assistance will have demonstrably bad effects, either on the economy, through limiting the capital available for investment, or on the unemployed themselves, through depriving them of their initiative or their self-respect. All such assertions are clearly empirical in reference, although so sweeping as to be extremely difficult to establish conclusively.

For reasons which are not clear, Runciman does not pursue this line of thinking in his essay. Instead, he seems to accept the conclusion expressed by Weber in discussing an imaginary debate between Schmoller and Babeuf. "If we were to set these two to arguing," Runciman writes, "and provide them with any evidence that they might require, it could be safely predicted that they would continue to disagree no matter how much discussion of feasibility and consistency they had gone through."[14]

In one sense, this observation is certainly correct. Everyone has noticed how difficult it is for anyone who has developed a coherent political position to accept more than minor amendments in such a position as a result of chiding from antagonists. Everyone has no-

[14] Op. cit., p. 170.

ticed, too, how "evidence" bearing on such positions is apt to be doubted, disputed, reinterpreted and ignored by those who hold them. So, as a statement about two specific historical personalities and their likely behavior under hypothetical conditions, Runciman's comment is certainly fair.

But if one's concern lies more narrowly with the intellectual possibilities of the questions concerned, the judgment is different. The fact that given disputants may be unmoved by facts, or that no conceivable infusion of facts may suffice to change their minds, does not obviate the reality that they are arguing about factual questions. The empirical propositions embodied in any particular political philosophy may be far-reaching and difficult to prove conclusively, but they are nonetheless factual for all that.

For further evidence of the role of empirical issues in the clash of political philosophies, we need look no further than the sorts of justifications which people typically offer the positions they espouse. Few will be satisfied to state a favorite political doctrine as God-given or morally absolute and let the matter go at that. Instead, people typically offer "reasons" for their beliefs, reasons which, as I have argued, have to do with the purported desirability of the results stemming from their implementation. This seems to be what Runciman has in mind when he writes of a political discussion with an imaginary syndicalist:

> If . . . the syndicalist is to make any kind of move to justify his position, then he will have to make some such reply as that he believes all government to be evil. But as soon as he has done this, we shall ask him for evidence; and we shall thereby have embarked on just such a political-sociological discussion as may require him to modify his position.[15]

Does social science have a role in the intellectual collisions between such positions? Indeed it does, since, as Runciman points out, the debates often turn on precisely those issues which social scientists study. Moreover, there is reason to believe that public

[15] Ibid., pp. 158–159.

discourse on political questions is becoming increasingly mediated by social science language and reasoning. In other words, present-day political arguments seem more and more to cast the empirical component of their disputes in specific propositions which are accessible to analysis and criticism in social science terms.

Take, for example, Edward Banfield's book *The Unheavenly City*—as authentic a manifestation of conservative values as anything written by Edmund Burke. The book is an analysis of the social causes and the most promising cures of the "urban crisis" in America of the late 1960's. The key argument of *The Unheavenly City* is that most of the characteristic problems of city life are caused by the behavior of the lower class, and that such behavior stems from the distinctive psychological characteristics of lower-class people. He writes,

> . . . the lower-class individual lives from moment to moment.
> . . . Impulse governs his behavior, either because he cannot discipline himself to sacrifice a present for a future satisfaction or because he has no sense of the future. He is therefore radically improvident: whatever he cannot consume immediately he considers valueless. His bodily needs (especially for sex) and his taste for "action" take precedence over everything else. . . .
> . . . In his relations with others he is suspicious and hostile, aggressive yet dependent. He is unable to maintain a stable relationship with a mate; commonly he does not marry. He feels no attachment to community, neighbors, or friends . . . resents all authority (for example, that of policemen, social workers, teachers, landlords, employers), and is apt to think that he has been "railroaded" and to want to "get even." He is a nonparticipant: he belongs to no voluntary organizations, has no political interests, and does not vote unless paid to do so.[16]

The tone of the passage—and the value positions from which it springs—are hardly different from those adopted by Burke toward

[16] (Boston: Little, Brown and Co., 1968), p. 53.

the French revolutionaries. Nor is the *sociological analysis* in Banfield's passage really new—i.e., his view of the poor as a disorganized rabble, responsible for their own degradation and liable to undermine the foundations of organized civilization if not held in check. These are classical tenents of conservative thinking, manifest in the writing of Burke, Taine, Le Bon, and countless others.

But Banfield's book was written in 1968, and the author couched its arguments in social science discourse. These facts make it possible to deal with the book in terms of the systematic appraisal of its empirical arguments, rather than simply as a unique expression of one man's reactions. Banfield's arguments take their place in a much wider array of statements by specialists on the social conditions of urban life; its empirical arguments thus face much more systematic scrutiny than did, say, those quoted above by Edmund Burke. Sophisticated critics do not simply decry the value positions embraced by Banfield, but instead draw on the accumulated evidence of research to attack his empirical assertions. Peter Rossi, for example, dealt with the Banfield argument in the following terms:

> There is nothing but the most fragmentary and inconclusive evidence that there is a "lower class" which is unable to defer gratification, or plan for the future. Furthermore there is even less evidence for the existence of a "permanent lower class," households and individuals who have descended from a line of lower class ancestors. The best empirical studies of American social stratification are not cited.[17]

Social science organizes inquiry on important empirical questions and provides systems for critically evaluating new findings and conclusions. By so doing, it can contribute to the resolution of clashes between contending political philosophies.

No one would doubt that Banfield's arguments, or any other politically charged assertions, express distinctive value preferences on the part of those who make them. In debates over educational

[17] "The City as Purgatory," *Social Science Quarterly* (March, 1971), Vol. LI, No. 4, p. 818.

policy, for example, proponents of conservative, traditional peda-
gogy will likely regard self-discipline and restraint as cardinal personal virtues; progressives, on the other hand, will place higher
value on spontaneity and self-expression. But neither party is apt
to win much public support unless it can show that the application
of these virtues, in specific educational ventures, can bring specific
desirable results. Thus arguments for particular approaches to
schooling typically stress that their implementation helps students
to read or write sooner, or to develop greater interest in their studies. Unless the proponents of such philosophies can make such empirical arguments persuasive to those who do not share their ultimate values, their preachments will satisfy only those already
converted. The *instrumental* value of such approaches, rather than
the ultimate values embodied in them, will matter most in their
success or failure in winning the crucial "middle ground" of public opinion. And social science thinking can make substantial contributions to assessing such instrumental values.

Nor is this the only way in which empirical arguments can help
to evaluate the claims of political doctrine and mediate the clash
of political world views. Often we find that such comprehensive
political viewpoints take as axiomatic certain interpretations of the
working of the social world. An example might be the assumption,
common to many left-wing positions, that important political
events and conditions stem from machinations of a selfish elite
or the workings of a sinister "system." Another might be the common assumption of conservative thinkers that social order represents a fragile product, liable to be disturbed by any weakening of
the state. These assumptions clearly have an empirical reference.
Though it may be very difficult to get people to agree as to what
might constitute adequate evidence to bear on them, such evidence
must in principle exist.

Yet another form of empirical discussion which may help resolve political questions has to do with the *implementation* of political values. It often happens that people of otherwise different

political persuasions find themselves, perhaps to their embarrass-
ment, espousing what appear to be identical ultimate values. Such
encounters set the stage for interesting empirical debates. "But
really," one contestant will say, "if you claim to believe in complete equality of opportunity, you must agree with me that the
democratic welfare state is the only acceptable form of government." "Hardly," we might imagine the other saying; "for the
welfare state only provides for equal treatment of those whose contributions to society are unequal. *True* equality of opportunity can
be realized only under unrestrained free enterprise." In the en-
suing disputes, the contestants may determine that their ultimate
values really are rather different after all—but not necessarily. The
discussions may prove to turn on important empirical points, such
as the amount of social mobility afforded under the systems in
question, or the degrees of freedom in consumption habits which
might be enjoyed under each. Social science insight would have a
real contribution to make to the empirical components of such
debates.

THE LIMITS OF EMPIRICAL MEDIATION

Do I mean to suggest, then, that the application of social science
promises a quick and complete resolution to the empirical issues
embodied in the clash of political philosophies? Such a conclusion
would be foolish. The empirical ideas embodied in such positions
tend to be sweeping and diffuse, and to that extent difficult to dis-
till into any one single set of researchable propositions. Moreover, the findings of empirical research, even with regard to
discrete points of fact, are notoriously subject to disputed interpretations among those with differing value predispositions. Thus,
disputes over such basically factual but highly value-relevant issues
as the past success of socialist versus capitalist strategies for developing economies are scarcely candidates for quick, decisive
resolution.

Moreover, many clashes of value orientation entail no serious empirical differences at all, and these include many of the most drastic differences. One can reasonably expect empirical analysis to help clarify the debates between environmentalists and industrialists concerning public policy on environmental matters; after all, the question of the total *effects* of a particular policy is often crucial in such cases. But no amount of empirical analysis could mitigate an opposition such as that between American Indians and the first white settlers as to how the North American environment should be exploited. In some sense, this conflict entailed a clash of values as to whether the indigenous hunting and gathering economy or European-style agriculture and commerce represented a morally preferable relationship between man and nature. And sociological analysis is as irrelevant to the resolution of issues like these as Weber claimed it was.

But fortunately, the clashes of political doctrine which bombard most of us most of the time are not like this. Much more common are what amount to disputes among contending programs for social arrangements in the complex industrial societies in which we live. This is not to say that such disputes are simply, as Runciman put it, debates over different ways of accomplishing the same things. But our discussions of politics and society do embody assertions and assumptions about matters of fact, and about cause-effect relations, which are in principle empirically verifiable. Social scientists can make a real contribution by dividing such debates into their empirical and metaphysical elements. To the latter, we can apply efforts like the "sympathetic exegesis" envisaged by Runciman—though with no absolute guarantee of success. To the empirical disputes, we can apply the most hard-headed social science analysis that we can, however difficult and frustrating we know such debates to be.

4

Ideology—Can We Do Without It?
A Critique of Karl Popper and
Dogmatic Moderation

This chapter has two goals: first, to identify an intellectual mood; second, to analyze and criticize doctrines which give expression to this mood. The mood is the widespread antipathy among social scientists to sweeping indictments of the status quo in Western democracies and to fundamental proposals for social change. The doctrines are those which hold all such interpretations and programs not only ill-founded but also inherently misguided and indeed "irrational." The chapter focuses mainly on the writings of Karl Popper, who has put forward the most sophisticated justifications of these positions.

IDEOLOGY AND UTOPIAN PLANNING

Even by the standards of disciplines not noted for terminological rigor, "ideology" must be one of our looser notions. The term has come to be used so generally as to mean any comprehensive social or political world view, especially one justifying a particular social position or interest. Within this very broad characterization, as Nathan Glazer has pointed out, the word is used in the widest array of meanings, running from laudatory to pejorative.[1]

Among contemporary middle-of-the-road social scientists, the term has virtually become an epithet—the epitome of all that the honest search for truth ought to foreswear. Ideological thinking, in this view, represents a way of looking at social life which is at once extreme, doctrinaire, and closed-minded. Thus, Edward Shils writes, in his article on ideology in the *International Encyclopedia of the Social Sciences:*

> The ideological culture . . . [interferes] with the attainment of truth. This is . . . a result of the closure of the ideological disposition to new evidence and its distrust of all who do not share the same ideological disposition. The chief source of tension between ideology and truth lies, therefore, in the concurrent demands of the exponents of ideologies for unity of belief and disciplined adherence on the part of their fellow believers. Both of these features of the ideological orientation make for dogmatic inflexibility and unwillingness to allow new experience to contribute to the growth of truth.[2]

Now, given that Shils begins by defining ideology as a prejudiced, non-veridical point of view, one might hold that this statement is no less than consistent with his original premises. But it gives one pause to note that, in the same article, he identifies Marxism as ideological, noting that "It is true that the social sciences have absorbed and domesticated bits of ideologies . . . but they themselves have seldom been ideological. Insofar as the social sciences have been genuinely intellectual pursuits . . . they are antipathetic to ideology."[3]

[1] "The Ideological Uses of Sociology," in Paul Lazarsfeld et al., *The Uses of Sociology* (New York: Basic Books, Inc., 1967), pp. 63–77.

[2] VII, 74.

[3] Ibid. Another version of this position is to be found in Robert Lane, "The Decline of Politics and Ideology in a Knowledgeable Society," *American Sociological Review* (October, 1966), Vol. XXXI, No. 5.

One wonders. It seems rash to characterize the thinking of, let us say, Marx, Gramsci, and Hobsbawm as "closed to new evidence and distrustful of all who do not share the same ideological orientation," while apparently excusing "non-ideological" writers like Durkheim, Park, or Parsons from such limitations. Nevertheless, Shils's position has much support from other influential defenders of the political and sociological center. We might recall, for example, the statement quoted in Chapter One by Daniel Bell and Irving Kristol from their editorial manifesto on the founding of their journal, *The Public Interest:*

> Thus, we must admit—or, if you wish, assert—that . . . [our] emphasis is not easily reconcilable with a prior commitment to an ideology, whether it be liberal, conservative, or radical. For it is the nature of ideology to *preconceive* reality; and it is exactly such preconceptions that are the worst hindrances to knowing-what-one-is-talking-about. It goes without saying that human thought and action is impossible without *some kinds* of preconceptions. . . . But it is the essential peculiarity of ideologies that they do not simply prescribe ends but also insistently propose prefabricated interpretations of existing social realities—interpretations that bitterly resist all sensible revision. THE PUBLIC INTEREST will be animated by a bias against all such prefabrications.[4]

In one sense, of course, the point is trivial. It is meaningless to oppose "prefabricated interpretations . . . that resist all sensible revision" and "dogmatic inflexibility and unwillingness to allow new experiences to contribute to the growth of truth" because no one advocates such things. But Shils, Bell, and Kristol seem to mean something more than this. They seem to suggest that their own techniques of analysis or axioms of thought are open-minded, fair, and reasonable, while the thinking of those who embrace other doctrines is flawed from the start by their having in some sense made up their minds in advance.

[4] Number 1, Fall, 1965, pp. 3–4.

Agree with this position or not, it would be hard to underestimate its significance for the concerns of this book. For the arguments of Bell, Kristol, Lane, Shils, and the other anti-ideologists embody an important and influential message on the role of social science insight in social betterment. As practicing social scientists, these writers have helped shape an expanded role for social science in policy making. Indeed, they have been among the most influential of the "social problem solvers" discussed in Chapter One. But their credo has always been determinedly moderate: "Analyze the workings of society as it is, and let your analyses inspire suggestions for social change," they seem to be telling us, "but do not contemplate any radical plans, any fundamental rearrangements of social structure." The use of social insight to improve the existing system is rational and scientific, they seem to feel. But to entertain possibilities for sweeping departures from the status quo apparently smacks of ideology and unreason.

What are we to make of this doctrine? Does it represent sound advice to the social scientist wishing to predicate plans for social intervention on the fairest, most "scientific" premises? Or is it merely a manifestation of its proponents' political prejudices? These are difficult questions to settle, for the anti-ideological persuasion asserts itself more often as a mood than as a full-blown doctrine. But the doctrine—at least one variant of it—has had one brilliant exponent in Sir Karl Popper.

Popper, to be sure, differs from the other writers mentioned above in many respects. European rather than American, a philosopher rather than a social scientist, Popper has apparently neither influenced nor been influenced by the others. We cannot be sure whether they would always accept his arguments as adequate defenses of their positions. But Popper's position embodies what I would consider the key elements of the anti-ideological approach— skepticism of fundamental indictments of the social order of Western democracies and of sweeping plans for social change, and rejection of the thought patterns underlying such tendencies as "irrational." True, the language of the arguments may differ. Popper terms the offending thought forms "utopian social planning," while the Americans, as we have seen, are more likely to condemn "ideological thinking." But the underlying dissatisfactions are the same, and Popper's justification of the intellectual mood which all share is the most comprehensive and sophisticated available.

POPPER'S PROGRAM FOR "RATIONAL" SOCIAL AMELIORATION

Of all living thinkers, Popper comes closest to being an official spokesman for parliamentary and libertarian institutions. A refugee from fascism and a disenchanted former Marxist, Popper has developed in his social writings a comprehensive attack on the intellectual bases of the political extremes. A pervasive theme in his writings is the defense of progressive improvement in social conditions through reasoned analysis. Plans for such progressive action, he argues, must emerge from the give-and-take of open public discussion.

In all his arguments, Popper insists that social planning, in order to be "rational," must be moderate and incremental. He resolutely opposes sweeping, comprehensive designs for fundamental social or political rearrangements—opposes them presumably even when they originate from duly constituted, democratic political institutions. He devotes much of his social writings to describing and criticizing these "holistic" forms of social planning:

> Holistic or Utopian social engineering . . . is never of a "private" but always of a "public" character. It aims at remodeling the "whole of society" in accordance with a definite plan or blueprint . . . it aims, furthermore, at controlling . . . the historical forces that mould the future of the developing society. . . .[5]

[5] *The Poverty of Historicism* (3rd ed., New York: Basic Books, 1960), p. 67.

His attitude toward this approach is unvaryingly critical:

> What I criticize under the name Utopian engineering recommends the reconstruction of society as a whole, i.e. very sweeping changes whose practical consequences are hard to calculate, owing to our limited experiences.[6]

Against the Utopian approach, Popper counterposes his famous alternative of "piecemeal social engineering":

> The characteristic approach of the piecemeal engineer is this. Even though he may perhaps cherish some ideals which concern society "as a whole"—its general welfare, perhaps—he does not believe in the method of re-designing it as a whole. Whatever his ends, he tries to achieve them by small adjustments and re-adjustments which can be continually improved upon.[7]

Popper regards the piecemeal method as the mark of rationality in the effort at social betterment. He offers two broad arguments as to why this is so. First, he holds that more ambitious plans exceed what is justified by our present limited understanding of social life. Second, he asserts that the very extent of such plans makes it difficult to assess their success or failure:

> The piecemeal engineer knows, like Socrates, how little he knows. He knows that we can only learn from our mistakes. Accordingly, he will make his way, step by step, carefully comparing the results expected with the results achieved, and always on the look-out for the unavoidable unwanted consequences of any reform; and he will avoid undertaking reforms of a complexity and scope which make it impossible for him to disentangle causes and effects, and to know what he is really doing.[8]

The arguments are developed at many points in Popper's social writings; in one criticism of Utopian methods, he notes:

[6] *The Open Society and Its Enemies* (Princeton, N.J.: Princeton University Press, 1963), Vol. I, p. 161.
[7] *The Poverty of Historicism,* p. 66.
[8] Ibid., p. 67.

It claims to plan rationally for the whole of society, although we do not possess anything like the factual knowledge which would be necessary to make good such an ambitious claim. We cannot possess such knowledge since we have insufficient practical experience in this kind of planning, and knowledge of facts must be based upon experience. At present, the sociological knowledge necessary for large-scale engineering is simply non-existent.[9]

Popper seems to address his remarks to all persons of good will who sincerely desire a better social world; he does not have much to say explicitly about the role of social scientists. By implication, however, they have an important part to play in Popper's program. For as specialists in social understanding, they ought to be especially capable of developing and evaluating piecemeal plans. And they should be particularly critical of plans which exceed Popper's safe limit of established social understanding.

THE GOALS OF PIECEMEAL INTERVENTION

How are we to appraise Popper's piecemeal technique? How far does it take us in dealing with the problems encountered by other doctrines examined in this book?

A key issue for any theory of social betterment is the specification of the *ends* of ameliorative action. What does it *mean* to improve social conditions? How does the rational social planner select goals for his or her efforts? In answering these questions, Popper often relies upon a simple-minded "social problems" view like those discussed in Chapter One. "I think that we should welcome any suggestion as to how our problems might be solved," he says at one point, "regardless of the atttitude towards society of the man who puts them forward."[10]

But, as we have seen, this ingenuous approach raises some em-

[9] *The Open Society and Its Enemies,* Vol. I, pp. 161–162.
[10] "Reason or Revolution?," Theodor W. Adorno, et. al., *The Positivist Dispute in German Sociology* (English ed., New York: Harper & Row, Inc., 1976), p. 298.

barrassing questions. Who is to designate what is "problematic"?
What if "problems" for one element of society represent just and
desirable conditions for others? Popper does not engage these
questions, but often seems to hold that the goals of social change
are, or at least ought to be, self-evident. When he offers examples
of ameliorative measures which he favors, they turn out to be
standard, middle-of-the-road social reforms:

> . . . the introduction, whether by a private or a public insur-
> ance company, of a new type of health or employment insur-
> ance; or the introduction of a new sales tax, or of a policy to
> combat trade cycles.[11]

The scale of the reforms cited in this and other of Popper's examples corresponds well with the piecemeal principles noted above.
Nevertheless, he refuses on principle to give a formula for specifying the ultimate ends of planned social change. He seems to hold
that such specification is both impractical and logically tenuous. On
much the same grounds as Weber, he seems to believe that the
evaluation of ultimate values is, in Popper's words, "largely beyond the power of *scientific* argument."[12]

But if unwilling to commit himself on the specification of ultimate ends, Popper does offer a practical, *ad hoc* rationale for the
goals of social intervention. It is a formula which he seems to feel
forestalls the need for more abstract considerations:

> Work for the elimination of concrete evils rather than for the
> realization of abstract goods . . . aim at the elimination of
> concrete miseries. . . . Choose what you consider the most
> urgent evil of the society in which you live, and try patiently
> to convince people that we can get rid of it.[13]

Popper evidently regards this approach as much less problematic
than any attempt to specify the long-term directions of social
change. He writes:

[11] *The Poverty of Historicism,* p. 86.
[12] *Conjectures and Refutations* (New York: Basic Books, 1963), p. 359.
[13] Ibid., p. 361.

> It is a fact, and not a very strange fact, that it is not so very difficult to reach agreement by discussion on what are the most intolerable evils of our society, and on what are the most urgent social reforms. . . . For the evils are with us here and now. They can be experienced, and are being experienced every day, by many people who have been and are being made miserable by poverty, unemployment, national oppression, war and disease.[14]

The sense of this position—not made explicit in Popper's own words, so far as I know—seems to be this: We have no logical way of proving the worth of any given set of *ultimate* social ends. But most people, as a matter of fact, share the instinct of combatting concrete miseries as a *worthy short-term* end. This interpretation at least fits well with Popper's predilection for modest, step-at-a-time reform.

The trouble with this position is simply that it is very implausible. Dispute over what constitutes "the most intolerable evils of our society" in fact represents the stock-in-trade of political controversy. Far from being a matter of consensus, "the most urgent social reforms" are the subject of endless discordant interpretations. Which measure promises to avail more in the alleviation of misery—a tax break for industry to raise the level of employment or reduction of personal income tax? Which is more compelling, the case for longer prison sentences for violent criminals, as a protection to the public; or that for more lenient treatment of the criminals themselves, in hopes of their rehabilitation? All of these possibilities aim at the reduction of *someone's* misery, and all fit Popper's standard of piecemeal technique. But I suspect that, if anything, it would be easier to establish general agreement over very abstract, somewhat vague, long-term goals like justice, freedom, equality, etc., than over these concrete, short-term policy matters. And this is scarcely to say that agreement over the former would be easy.

[14] Ibid.

HOW PIECEMEAL IS PIECEMEAL?

But this is only the beginning of Popper's difficulties in fitting his theories to the demands of practice. For when we examine closely his most basic distinction between piecemeal and holistic planning, we find serious ambiguities. Indeed, Popper seems unwilling or unable to draw a clear distinction between the two.

Often Popper characterizes objectionable forms of planning as those aiming at ". . . remodeling the 'whole of society' in accordance with a definite plan or blueprint."[15] Yet I doubt that even the most radical planner would espouse such intentions as more than a rhetorical flourish. True, many would prefer much more sweeping plans for social reform than those which Popper cherishes. Radicals wish to revamp whole complexes of institutions or reshape basic social structures; they may seek the sweeping democratization of political power or the rearrangement of work or educational institutions. But anyone literally seeking to revamp the *whole* of society would have to change everything from linguistic conventions to kinship systems at a blow. Such intentions are not integral to any radical plan for social reform that I know of.

But the ambition to change "the whole of society" is not the only characterization Popper gives to the forms of planning which he finds objectionable. Elsewhere, he directs his criticism against planning which is simply "too sweeping"—e.g., which goes beyond what is justified by established social understanding. But he remains unwilling to tell us just how sweeping is *too* sweeping. "I do not suggest that piecemeal engineering cannot be bold, or that it must be confined to 'smallish' problems," he states, "But I think that the degree of complication which we can tackle is governed by the degree of our experience gained in conscious and systematic piecemeal engineering."[16] But he gives no systematic ac-

---

[15] *The Poverty of Historicism*, p. 67.
[16] *The Open Society and Its Enemies*, Vol. I, p. 285.

count of how one might reckon the degree of complication in planning warranted by any particular amount of past experience.

The point is no quibble. Unless it can be resolved, Popper's position becomes nothing more than an evocation of the anti-ideological mood. After all, no one social situation is ever *exactly* identical to any other. Any application of insight drawn from one setting to another involves some element of abstraction and generalization—in short, some "theory." The question of how analysis of past experience and events can form the intellectual basis for future social intervention challenges both Popper's piecemeal doctrines and all other formulae for insight in the service of social betterment.

These ambiguities in Popper's position become especially perplexing in the light of his well-known epistemological doctrines. In one of the passages cited above, he characteristically states his objections to sweeping projects for change in terms of the lack of ". . . *factual knowledge* which would be necessary to make good such an ambitious claim." "We cannot possess such knowledge since we have insufficient practical experience in this kind of planning . . ." he continues.[17] But Popper would be the last to argue that any amount of experience automatically "accumulates" to constitute knowledge. For him, the growth of knowledge comes through the thinker's advancing new and more comprehensive hypotheses—"conjectures," to use his famous term—to be either confirmed or refuted in the encounter with empirical evidence. In the case of social planning, Popper seems to be advising us to keep our conjectures, in the form of inspirations for social innovation, as close as possible to precedent. But again, he gives no formula for how close this must be in practice.

Popper finally acknowledges his inability to specify the principles underlying his preferences. Nevertheless, like many an art lover, he "knows what he likes":

---

[17] Ibid., pp. 161–62. The emphasis is my own.

It may be questioned, perhaps, whether the piecemeal and the holistic approaches here described are fundamentally different, considering that we have put no limits to the scope of a piecemeal approach. As this approach is understood here, constitutional reform, for example, falls well within its scope; nor shall I exclude the possibility that a series of piecemeal reforms might be inspired by one general tendency, for example, a tendency towards a greater equalization of incomes. . . .

In answering this question, I shall not attempt to draw a precise line of demarcation between the two methods. . . .[18]

So far as I can determine, no workable "line of demarcation" is developed anywhere in Popper's writing.

POPPER'S FLIGHT FROM SOCIAL THEORY

This anomaly, I believe, points to a very serious shortcoming of Popper's overall approach. That is his refusal to provide any systematic judgment of the social forces creating and perpetuating undesirable social conditions. He turns his back, in other words, precisely on what Barrington Moore pursues with such searing honesty—examination of the "causes of human misery."[19]

Instead, Popper offers us a weak and simplistic approach to social intervention—what I would call an "additive model" of human suffering. He advises us to attack "our problems" or "concrete human miseries" as directly as possible, without any reckoning of their contextual role in the larger social whole. He implausibly implies that "the most intolerable evils" of society are unconnected to one another, that efforts at their alleviation require no over-arching analysis of larger social forces generating the offending conditions.

This is very unsatisfactory. Nearly everyone would agree, for example, that not all forms of human suffering represent equally appropriate targets for corrective action. Enormous amounts of inter-

[18] *The Poverty of Historicism,* p. 68.
[19] Barrington Moore, Jr., *Reflections on the Causes of Human Misery* (Boston: Beacon Press, 1972).

personal suffering occur within the family, for example—through symbolic cruelty, thoughtlessness, and the like. Yet people regard many of these and other acute forms of misery as outside the scope of social reform. Either they strike us as inevitable or they do not seem susceptible to social intervention—perhaps because really effective measures would violate other values, such as privacy. Any plan for attacking human suffering must entail complicated calculations both of the social forces generating such conditions and of the social and ethical considerations bearing on the effectiveness of ameliorative measures.

A great deal of human misery, one supposes, takes place in prisons. But one doubts that Popper or anyone else would advocate throwing open all prison gates as a promising measure of piecemeal reform. We would reject such a measure on the grounds that it would entail, on balance, distinctly undesirable *effects*. That is, it would cause unacceptable suffering for other members of society or would obviate the deterrent example of punishment. The example is simplistic, but it illustrates the need for sociological analysis in any scheme for social betterment. The direct alleviation of any one form of misery may result in greater miseries in the future or elsewhere in society. And the alleviation of any one form of suffering may best be accomplished by attacking what at first seem distant and unrelated social conditions which, on examination, prove influential in its causation.

Popper's approach provides no help at all in dealing with these issues. His strategy specifically discourages us from considering some entirely plausible sociological hypotheses—for example, the possibility that concentration of power in the hands of an elite may represent a key condition for all sorts of unnecessary suffering. Indeed, it appears that such analyses of major causal orderings are precisely what Popper deplores as "holistic thinking" and "blueprints for society as a whole."

But if social science teaches us anything, it should alert us at least to the possibility of over-arching yet non-intuitive causation in society. It would take a naïve piecemeal planner indeed to approach an economic depression as a co-occurrence of discrete and unrelated slowdowns in thousands of different enterprises. On the contrary, any reasonable analysis of such a situation, and any plan for its cure, must be somehow holistic—that is, must deal with forces affecting the overall relation of all parts of the economy to one another. Similarly, we have no reason to reject outright the possibility that fundamental changes in social relations—say, the drastic equalization of power among different social groupings— may represent an essential step in alleviating misery.

The United States has probably institutionalized more "piecemeal social engineering" than any other country in the world. Nowhere else, to my knowledge, is there such a proliferation of discrete, heterogeneous plans for combatting "social problems" or such a lack of intellectual or organizational coherence in the efforts against them. Everyone knows that one of our most celebrated social problems is poverty. An account of the reasoned discussions, theorizing, and piecemeal experiments on this subject just over the last fifteen years would fill volumes. Yet, as the Scriptures tell us, the poor remain with us, and chronic poverty in America persists stubbornly at levels excessive even by the standards of other capitalist systems.

Now, one need scarcely be an ideologue to point out that the high levels of chronic poverty in America have much to do with the fact that unemployment has rarely dropped below 4 percent in the last two decades—a level which would be unacceptable to powerful working-class interests in other developed capitalist countries. Nor is this level of unemployment itself an accident. It is generally agreed that planners at the highest level of government and business seek to maintain these levels. Their role in curbing wage demands is an important element of top-level planning.

I suppose that Popper would applaud the American approach to the "poverty problem"—much reasoned discussion, endless discrete experiments, and virtually no "holistic" efforts aimed at drastic reduction of unemployment. But the powerful figures in government and industry who manipulate unemployment levels to serve larger political and economic ends have no hesitation in their recourse to sweeping, comprehensive plans. Nor will piecemeal efforts to combat poverty do much good until those who hold real power come to regard full employment as acceptable to their interests—or, until those who regard full employment as acceptable and desirable come to power. Not any open competition among ideas about poverty, but the contest of social interests involved in poverty-producing conditions, will shape the outcome of this particular struggle against human suffering.

Popper frequently insists that we ". . . avoid undertaking reforms of a complexity and scope which make it impossible . . . to disentangle causes and effects, and to know what . . . [we are] really doing."[20] And no doubt, it is true that the results of very large experiments may be difficult to interpret. Yet, in cases such as poverty, really fundamental conditions of human misery may only be susceptible to manipulation through very far-reaching social experiments. We have no *a priori* justification for believing that the origins of suffering must necessarily represent the additive results of many discrete, separable causes, or that the causes of human misery, whatever they are, can necessarily be broken down into incremental units for piecemeal change. All that we know for certain is that some conditions respond to congeries of discrete, separable causes and others to pervasive, holistic ones. There is nothing inherently irrational about positing fundamental rearrangements or qualitatively new approaches as possibilities for sweeping and effective social change.

Yet Popper inveighs against this possibility consistently. For example,

> The Utopian engineer will of course claim that mechanical engineers sometimes plan even very complicated machinery as

[20] *The Poverty of Historicism*, p. 67.

a whole, and that their blueprints may cover, and plan in advance, not only a certain kind of machinery, but even the whole factory which produces this machinery. My reply would be that the mechanical engineer can do all this because he has sufficient experience at his disposal, i.e. theories developed by trial and error. But this means that he can plan because he has made all kinds of mistakes already; or in other words, because he relies on experience which he has gained by applying piecemeal methods.[21]

The statement is dogmatic. While some scientific and technological innovations seem to develop incrementally, others reflect striking departures from past practice, based on new theoretical insights. The possibilities of harnessing atomic energy, after all, became apparent only through abstract theoretical inquiry. These sweeping changes in theoretical understanding finally gave rise to qualitatively new experiments—the first controlled nuclear reaction or the first atomic explosion. We cannot reject the possibility that social innovation may proceed in the same way.

THE POLITICAL BIAS OF POPPER'S "OPEN-MINDEDNESS"

Perhaps the most forceful and significant of Popper's claims for his doctrines is that they alone embody a rational approach to social betterment. He condemns alternative views as not only wrong but fundamentally unscientific:

> . . . while the piecemeal engineer can attack his problem with an open mind as to the scope of the reform, the holist cannot do this; for he has decided beforehand that a complete reconstruction is possible and necessary. This fact has far-reaching consequences. It prejudices the Utopianist against certain sociological hypotheses which state limits to institutional control. . . . By a rejection *a priori* of such hypotheses, the Utopian approach violates the principles of scientific method.[22]

[21] *The Open Society and Its Enemies,* Vol. I, p. 163.
[22] *The Poverty of Historicism,* p. 69.

As we have seen, Popper shares this position with the American antagonists of "ideological thinking." The preceding passage recalls the words of Shils, who writes:

> The ideological culture . . . [interferes] with the attainment of truth. This is . . . a result of the closure of the ideological disposition to new evidence and its distrust of all who do not share the same ideological disposition.[23]

I have tried to show that arguments like these can just as well be turned against those who fashion them. It is Popper who displays prejudice when he argues, *a priori,* for the rejection of holistic analyses of social misery and sweeping measures for its alleviation. Popper's position in these respects is no less dogmatic than a radical's categorical refusal to entertain arguments that revolution might not, indeed, automatically bring about the changes which he might desire. The nature of the forces shaping human welfare, and particularly their discrete versus their holistic character, are hardly matters for categorical assumption. Only empirical inquiry and reasoned debate can promise to yield any conclusions about them. Popper's refusal to entertain possibilities which he obviously dislikes hardly displays the "open-mindedness" which he claims for his position.

This disingenuousness points to an important feature of Popper's doctrines—their covert, but highly significant, political content. His claims of open-mindedness notwithstanding, Popper arbitrarily rules out entirely reasonable possibilities associated with radical perspectives on social change. Instead, he embraces positions long associated with conservative and centrist doctrines. These latter assumptions, which play such an influential role in his positions, demand explicit identification.[24]

[23] Edward Shils, *loc. cit.*

[24] Popper's idea that social planning may easily make things worse by exceeding the scope of incrementally developed human understanding, for example, has a long pedigree in conservative thought. Note the similarities, say, to the arguments in Michael Oakeshott, *Rationalism in Politics* (New York: Basic Books, Inc., 1967).

One such assumption lies in Popper's inordinate optimism concerning the openness of social systems to progressive change. "Choose what you consider the most urgent evil of the society in which you live, and try patiently to convince people that we can get rid of it,"[25] he advises us. Here Popper clearly would have us believe that those with power in any given society will necessarily want to take advantage of possibilities for reducing misery.

Perhaps the most generous thing to be said about this assumption is that it reflects a touching faith in the powers both of reason and of human good will. Chapter Two considered a number of persuasive arguments, including those of Herbert Gans, showing how powerful interests actually profit from human suffering and seek its continuation. I have argued just above that unemployment, though "problematic" to the unemployed and to certain social planners, profits the interests of those who have the greatest say in these things. No one may regard unemployment, or any number of other causes of human misery, as good things in themselves. But those in power may well find the suffering they entail a price well worth paying in exchange for the concomitant benefits—particularly if they are not the ones to pay. Popper's idea that the intellectual appeal of effective steps to the alleviation of misery will necessarily prevail over the opposition of forces like these, in a sort of free competition of ideas, reflects a faith that borders on naïveté. Certainly it betrays a systematic refusal to recognize the role of power in social systems. All of these assumptions are characteristic of conservative and centrist arguments, and they are hardly the easiest of such arguments to defend.

Nor are these the only ones of Popper's basic assumptions which, on examination, bristle with partisan political content. Another has to do with the *costs* of moderate *versus* decisive change. In one of his most often repeated arguments, Popper proclaims his approach to social betterment as the most economical of human suf-

[25] *Conjectures and Refutations,* p. 361.

fering. Stepwise, piecemeal planning, according to him, precludes the horrendous human costs likely to result from really sweeping innovations. "If they [piecemeal plans] go wrong," he writes, "the damage is not very great, and the readjustment is not very difficult."[26] By contrast, he characterizes more sweeping approaches as ". . . a method which, if really tried, may easily lead to an intolerable increase in human suffering."[27]

Certainly this position is no more than consistent with Popper's defense of parliamentary institutions and open deliberation in the formulation of plans for social betterment. By allowing plans for change to emerge from an open democratic forum, he contends, we forestall the risk that differences of opinion will break out into open conflicts that may actually cost lives:

> Critical debate is a method which permits our hypotheses to die for us—whereas the uncritical method of the fanatic demands that we testify as martyrs to our hypotheses: if they are faulty, we perish with them.[28]

The slogan of "letting our ideas die for us" is widely associated with Popper, and the theme recurs frequently in his writings on social betterment. "Keep talking, and keep listening to one another," he means to tell us, "for this will give the best chance for constructive change without bloodshed."

The trouble with all this is the assumption that inaction, or slowness or moderation in acting, must necessarily be cost-free. If human suffering is indeed to be alleviated, other things being equal, few would fail to agree that due process and maximum consensus are preferable to coercion as bases for the change. But we have no guarantee, I have argued, that those in power will accede to programs for the reduction of suffering, even after the most thorough exposition of their merits. Nor have we any guarantee that intoler-

---

[26] *The Open Society and Its Enemies,* Vol. I, p. 159.

[27] Ibid., p. 158.

[28] "On Reason and the Open Society," *Encounter* (May, 1972), Vol. XXXVIII, No. 5, p. 17.

able suffering, indeed widespread death and destruction, may not continue apace while "reasonable men" deliberate. And the risks of major human losses during the course of argumentation become especially great when, as is often the case in parliamentary regimes, those who do the deliberating stand at considerable social distance from those who do the suffering.

For clearly, suffering and death imposed by the status quo are no less authentic than those unleashed in the course of abrupt social change. Popper inveighs frequently against violence. He asserts the moral superiority of his own position on the grounds that alternative views must somehow embrace violence. But regimes which acquiesce to continuing losses of life through preventable diseases, industrial accidents, and the casualties of official repression must, as radical critics have often pointed out, bear the responsibility for this death toll in their own right.

The conservative assumption—Popper's assumption—cannot stand. Any reasoned approach to social betterment must embody examination of the *probable costs* of sweeping change *versus* those of deliberation. No one can doubt that such discussions must be difficult and trying. The stakes are inevitably highly emotional, and the calculations hypothetical and riddled with political content. But the alternative—to assume that drastic or coercive change has a monopoly on the creation of suffering—represents a monstrously insensitive approach to one of the subtlest political issues. It is an approach characteristic of conservative arguments, and a most unappealing one.

The political significance of assumptions like these is fairly clear, once they are examined. But beyond these points, some of the more subtle of Popper's orienting assumptions also merit comment. Throughout his social writings, Popper treats the intellectual calculations involved in social planning in much the same language as if he were discussing the growth of scientific knowledge. His attack on sweeping social plans, after all, emphasizes most of all the lack of a firm basis for such plans in established understanding. If the ideas underlying such plans were candidates for scientific acceptance, Popper seems to be telling us, they would require much more rigorous testing before they could be believed. They must receive this testing in the form of small-scale, piecemeal experiments before they are ready to be applied on a grand scale—if, indeed, it would ever be safe to make such sweeping applications.

But surely, the exigencies of practical politics and administration do not permit observance of the meticulous standards of certainty of scientific discourse. Popper is quite right to point out that many possible approaches to social betterment—indeed, perhaps all of them—rely on knowledge which is less than certain. Like the idea of "conjectures" in Popper's theory of knowledge, efforts at social change are never certain in their effects, but must await tentative confirmation or refutation by events in the real world. But the real world of political and social events is often a world of crisis and emergency, where even slender bases for action are preferable to none at all. Where lives are being lost or other precious resources being squandered, the rational political actor—moderate or radical—will not demand certainty in a plan to improve things. To demand certainty in such a situation would be much like refusing to jump from a burning building without first examining the credentials of the firemen holding the net below. Faced with a very pressing emergency, an untried plan with only a fifty-fifty chance of success may be preferable to inaction from almost any political viewpoint.

SOME REDEEMING INSIGHTS

I consider the shortcomings of Popper's positions so serious as to disqualify them as a *general method* for mobilizing understanding in the service of social betterment. Nevertheless, it would be a mistake to conclude that his observations have nothing to offer the concerns of this book. For some of his most important insights, stripped of their categorical expression, provide important cautions on the limitations and risks of social planning. Specifically, they remind us that nearly everyone would take a more cautious attitude toward the risks of very sweeping plans than to quite modest ones.

Amitai Etzioni has recently called attention to many of these same considerations.[29] What constitutes an "acceptable risk," he points out, depends very substantially on the seriousness of the damage, should the risk become a reality. A "small risk" of, say, one in one hundred may be entirely acceptable when the outcome is failing to get to the theatre on time for the performance. But the same level of risk may be entirely unacceptable when the undesired outcome is more serious—e.g., a risk to the safety of one's family.

Popper's arguments should help us keep in mind the implications of this principle for social planning. In academic discourse, we might regard a plan for social innovation as "promising" if it seemed to have no more than one chance in ten of failing. But the question is, how unacceptable are the consequences, should that one-in-ten risk materialize? If the failure of the plan with ninety percent probability of success were certain to cause widespread and unmitigated additional suffering for all concerned, then we might do well to reject even such a "promising" approach. The trouble with Popper on this point is simply that he assumes that *all* sweeping plans *must* entail this danger of added suffering, over and above the misery already embodied in the status quo.

---

[29] See his letter in the *New York Times Magazine* (March 24, 1974), p. 70. We must, he writes, ". . . fully take into account, in computing the risk-benefit of nuclear reactors, the size of the disutility. To say that reactors have a 1 out of 10,000 chance to blow each year (or 1 out of 1,000,000 per community), which makes them about as safe as flying, does not take into account the number of persons to be killed in a nuclear disaster. . . . Most persons who would accept a $10 bet at odds of 99 to 1 in their favor, would hesitate if the bet was $1000 at the *same* odds, and refuse a $100,000 bet at *identical* odds. Why? Only because the disutility changed."

We can draw a similar insight from Popper's warnings about short-term sacrifice in the interests of longer-term social betterment; he writes:

> . . . we must not argue that the misery of one generation may be considered as a mere means to the end of securing the lasting happiness of some later generation. . . . All generations are transient. All have an equal right to be considered, but our immediate duties are undoubtedly to the present generation and to the next.[30]

At first glance, this statement seems purely dogmatic. Surely, whether to favor the welfare of one's own generation or of one's grandchildren can only be a purely Weberian choice among ultimate values. Popper, like Weber, places this category of decision making largely beyond the realm of scientific debate.[31] Surely, then, he would seem to have no grounds for preaching his own preferences to the rest of us on this matter.

But there is a sense in which Popper's statement simply embodies a sound, common-sense principle which most of us would readily accept. Despite what he says, I suspect that many people would have no difficulty in accepting the principle of current self-denial on behalf of future generations, given *real certainty* that the hoped-for benefits would indeed materialize. We profess willingness, for example, to make present-day sacrifices in order to protect natural resources and ecological well-being for future generations. But the benefits arising from *not* tampering with the world as it is are much more certain than those supposed to stem from drastic sacrifices in order to build a new social order. The problem with sacrificing the comfort of one generation for the infinite happiness of subsequent ones is not just that we find the ultimate value choice unacceptable—although, indeed, we may. Rather, it is that we may have good reason to doubt the certainty of the eventual payoffs.

[30] *Conjectures and Refutations,* p. 362.
[31] Ibid., p. 359.

CONCLUSION

We should not hesitate to admire many of the values which Popper seeks to serve in his writings on social betterment. The twentieth century has seen more than its share of human misery, much of it self-imposed misery stemming from political or ideological conflicts. As Popper would be the first to point out, people have too often been willing to countenance such suffering, or, worse, to cause it, in hopes of serving some lofty "theoretical" goals. Under these circumstances, some have become inured to consider such human costs "inevitable" in social change; others take refuge in a conservatism that abhors constructive change altogether. Popper has done neither. He has attempted to find a role for reasoned planning for social betterment while guarding against the imposition of new suffering in the name of progress.

Nevertheless, our main concern lies with Popper's doctrines, rather than with the values which he means them to serve. Do his arguments successfully meet the challenges faced by other doctrines studied in this book? More specifically, do they fulfill the claim of providing the most "rational" approach to the relief of human suffering? I have argued that they do not. Ironically, the most serious failings of Popper's doctrine seem to lie in the *selectivity* of his application of rational judgment.

For the overall strategy which Popper recommends forecloses some of the most important issues facing any proponent of social betterment. He assumes, on the most superficial arguments, that fundamental, sweeping efforts at social change must necessarily risk greater suffering than that entailed in the status quo. He takes it for granted that those who hold power will readily accept the most effective plans for reducing human misery. He rejects *a priori* any analysis which might attribute to key groups or to basic social arrangements a paramount role in the generation of human suffering.

These are dogmatic positions, ones which unduly constrain

thinking on central issues facing any proponent of reasoned social betterment. I do not mean that Popper's conclusions need be wrong in every situation. I have argued, for example, that a rational approach to social betterment must *weigh* the likely costs in human suffering of plans for change against those of inaction. By the same token, the openness of elites to change, and the nature of the social forces generating human misery, can only be determined through the most thorough inquiry possible into the details of the situation at hand. Observers of different political identifications will certainly begin with their own distinctive preconceptions on these matters. But any *rational* examination of possibilities for constructive change requires critical appraisal of such preconceptions against the realities of the situation where change is contemplated. One can only make these calculations in terms of the specifics of given political and social situations. Yet Popper, like the most doctrinaire radical, has made up his mind in advance, once and for all.

Popper thus succeeds in narrowing the role of reason to piecemeal planning only at the cost of ruling out examination of really big issues. And it is significant that the issues which he chooses to ignore are the classical *political* questions. How open are social and political systems to significant evolutionary progressive change? Will drastic, abrupt social change necessarily tend to make things worse rather than better? These are issues which have long divided conservatives from liberals, moderates from radicals. Such questions are monumentally difficult, but this is hardly sufficient reason to skirt them.

Popper scarcely stands alone among the authors considered in this book in his attempt to avoid such political questions. Several have attempted to build formulae for social improvement which excuse the rational planner from considering the full range of political alternatives for change. Often this avoidance takes the form of refusing to examine critically the ends of social betterment. Myrdal, for example, insists that the planner can avoid imposing his or her own political goals by taking the values of the society under study as a guide. Merton develops a very similar position, claiming that the role of the social problem solver is strictly technical, that it does not involve imposing the social scientist's political views òn others. More generally, the rash of social problem-solving approaches discussed in Chapter One eschew consideration of major political issues and concentrate on smaller-scale social tinkering within existing political constraints.

All of these attempts, I have argued, fail. Indeed, it is precisely where writers attempt to avoid fundamental political questions that their arguments become unconvincing. For political realities set many of the most decisive conditions of social well-being. The distribution of power, wealth, and other scarce resources, the nature and rate of social change—fundamental questions like these are central to any attempt to improve the quality of social life. Any resolution of such questions decisively shapes the possibilities for social betterment. Any formula for rational improvement of social conditions which does not help us to address these difficult political choices falls short of the demands of the problem.

Chapter Three considered in some detail the contribution of social science thinking to fundamental political questions such as these. There, I argued that such questions are not purely matters of arbitrary choice among warring values, but that they also entail major empirical components susceptible to analysis through social science inquiry. The fact that such questions are extremely difficult in no way excuses us from attempting to deal with them. Indeed, social science can have no higher role in the rational improvement of social conditions than to engage these most fundamental of all issues.

5

The Frankfurt School:
Evaluation of Ultimate Ends

The history of social thought offers little in the way of authentic pathos. Weber's agonies over the dualism of fact and value, however, surely deserve such a designation. The calling of the scholar, in Weber's view, demanded examination of the mainsprings of social action—including the values which represented the end states of human striving. Yet Weber held that *empirical analysis* of ultimate values and of their role in social action could never warrant conclusions as to their ultimate worth. In this view, understanding the principles shaping social action confers no ability to help people decide how they *ought to live.* This irony both fired Weber's scholarly activities and agonized his spirit.

This issue is hardly less central to the concerns of this book than it was to Weber's life and work. I have tried to show how "social problems"—social conditions people might regard as ripe for improvement—actually represent clashes of value or interest. That is, they represent situations where one group or one set of interests stands to lose by others' gain. Thus, any enlightened intervention in such situations must seemingly require a partisan stand on behalf of one set of interests or values over against others. Yet if Weber was correct, social science stands powerless to justify such intervention.

Most people would count this a pessimistic conclusion. But certain more recent German philosophers and sociologists—members of the Frankfurt school—have attacked Weber's position as an abdication of the role of the intellectual. Max Horkheimer meant to indict both Weber and conventional social thought more generally when he complained,

> The view is abroad that reason is a useful instrument only for purposes of everyday life, but must fall silent in face of the great problems and give way to the more substantial powers of the soul. The result is the avoidance of any theoretical consideration of society as a whole.[1]

What Horkheimer means by "theoretical consideration of society as a whole" includes precisely what Weber held impossible—reasoned evaluation of the ultimate directions of social action. The willingness to make such evaluations—indeed, the insistence upon doing so—distinguishes this from other approaches to rational social betterment.

Critical Theorists, as these thinkers have been called, often dramatize the distinctiveness of their approach by contrasting it rather sweepingly to "positivistic" thinking. This usage can be misleading, since it lumps a heterogeneous array of approaches, many of whose exponents would not accept the designation "positivist." One focus of Critical Theorists' disapproval is the "social problem-solving approach" discussed in the first two chapters. The intellectual origins of this approach lie with Saint-Simon and Comte. Via Durkheim, Parsons, and Merton, it continues to have a major influence on empirical sociology, especially in America.

The distinguishing characteristic of this tradition, for our pur-

---

[1] *Critical Theory* (New York: Herder and Herder, 1972), p. 4.

pose, is to regard the ultimate ends of social action as settled and consensual. This makes it no more than logical to regard troublesome or undesirable social conditions as "social problems"—that is, as failures to attain end states which everyone really wants to reach. This assumption obviously opens the way for social scientists, as experts in the workings of societies, to provide what Merton calls "technical advice" on how better to attain such ends. At the same time, such thinking discourages attention to the *political* content of social problems.

We have already noted the antipathy of Weber's thinking to these assumptions. For him, there could be no strictly technical judgment of the rightness or wrongness of any social condition. Such judgments were meaningful only in terms of the values, including the political and ideological identifications, of the observer. The Frankfurt thinkers share Weber's position here. But they differ from Weber, as we have seen, in attacking the failure to allow for reasoned choice among values. They hold it absurd that the voice of reason should not be heard in deciding between such fundamental value alternatives as war and peace, exploitation and cooperation, or ignorance and enlightenment. The role of enlightened social inquiry, in their view, is to treat such choices not merely as matters of taste but as subjects of rational deliberation.

Clearly, then, the Critical Theorists offer a distinctive approach to the role of insight in social betterment. Their determination to entertain bases for choice among contending social values dramatically sets their position off from other doctrines considered in this book. The question is, is this position coherent and convincing?

THE EMERGENCE OF CRITICAL THEORY

Writing about Critical Theory is inevitably a precarious business. The following discussion deals first with the ideas of Max Horkheimer, Theodor Adorno, and Herbert Marcuse; these figures come close to embodying the essence of Critical Theory. Yet, the writings of these men range over a period of more than fifty years, from the early 1920's to the 1970's, and include some very disparate intellectual strains. All three share significant differences, in turn, from Jürgen Habermas, whose major writings have appeared since 1960. Discussion focuses separately on Habermas toward the end of this chapter.

What makes for special difficulty is the obscure and allusive quality of Critical Theorists' writing; here I include Habermas *a fortiori*. All four of these figures like to describe their position as a way of approaching issues rather than as a fixed body of doctrine. This is fair enough in itself, but it scarcely exempts these thinkers from taking stands on the hard issues confronting other approaches discussed in this book. We will have relatively little trouble discovering what Habermas and the Critical Theorists are *against*. The difficulty comes in interpreting their rather elusive statements about what intellectual alternatives they favor.

Critical Theory emerged in Germany during the late 1920's as an intellectual reaction to doctrinaire tendencies in established Marxism. The early Critical Theorists were disenchanted both with the role of Marxism in the authoritarian policies of the Soviet Union and with its development in the politically domesticated Social Democratic party in Germany. They objected to the idea of any fixed and "correct" interpretation of political realities. In contrast, the approach which they developed envisaged possibilities for social betterment as always "emergent," contingent on the encounter between living, reacting participants and unfolding social reality.

In the earliest period, Critical Theorists to some extent shared the standard Marxist faith in the proletariat as agent of "historical rationality." With the passage of time, however, their growing disappointment with working-class politics led them to reject the notion of any "inevitable" outcome to processes of historical development. Significantly, this new point of view placed the Critical Theorists close to the position of Karl Popper. What the Critical

Theorists came to oppose is much like what Popper termed "historicism"—the notion that understanding the "laws of history" enabled one to place oneself on the side of history's ultimate victors.

In *The Poverty of Historicism,* Popper demonstrated the far-reaching implications of this idea for political action. Among the most objectionable of these, he held, was the certainty that "history" would justify the most brutal short-term actions in the service of "inevitable" longer-term ends. Obviously this line of thinking presumes that people's efforts to shape their own social world can have no effect on the ultimately important forces of social change. Critical Theorists have joined Popper in attacking any scheme which does not recognize the potential role of active, thoughtful human beings in making their own history.

But elsewhere, Critical Theorists oppose Popper bitterly. Above all, they dispute Popper's contention that ameliorative social change must proceed by discrete, modest steps—his well known "piecemeal engineering" argument. Here, the contrast could not be sharper. For the interpretations fashioned by Critical Theory, and the implications of these interpretations for action, are relentlessly holistic. Far from advocating piecemeal tinkering with social forms, Critical Theorists regard the significance of any one element of social reality as wholly dependent on context. Adjustments or improvements to any single social institution, in their view, are liable to be futile without changes in the social whole.

Can one epitomize the essential approach of Critical Theory in a few words? One key assumption is that reasoned inquiry can always apprehend the shortcomings of established social reality and point ways to richer fulfillment of its potentials. Following Hegel, Critical Theorists believe that possibilities for enhanced realization of human potential struggle to be realized in every social and historical setting. But these potentials ordinarily can only find expression by breaking through the repressive limitations of the present order. Critical Theory should serve as a sort of intellectual instigator here; Horkheimer envisages its role as follows:

. . . its purpose is not . . . the better functioning of any element in the structure. On the contrary, it is suspicious of the very categories of better, useful, appropriate, productive, and valuable, as these are understood in the present order. . . . The critical attitude of which we are speaking is wholly distrustful of the rules of conduct with which society as presently constituted provides each of its members. The separation between individual and society in virtue of which the individual accepts as natural the limits prescribed for his activity is relativized in critical theory. The latter considers the overall framework which is conditioned by the blind interaction of individual activities (that is, the existent division of labor and the class distinctions) to be a function which originates in human action and therefore is a possible object of planful decision and rational determination of goals.[2]

If Hegel represents the intellectual grandfather of Critical Theory, then Marx is its father. Marx, Critical Theorists hold, struggled to identify and to overcome the repressive features of his own time. His critique of the irrationalities of early capitalism—for example, its bizarre juxtaposition of rational short-term planning and irrational boom-and-bust cycles—stands as a model of the critical method. But the task of critical reflection cannot be complete with Marx or anyone else. Every historical order embodies its own limitations on human potentials and its unique opportunities for breaking through those limitations. Significantly, Critical Theorists have been as ready to apply their method to the repressive features of left-oriented political movements and to socialist societies as to centrist and reactionary regimes. The underlying intent is deeply subversive, though not inherently militant or violent.

Thus, Critical Theorists seem to orient their work to different categories of "consumers" than do exponents of other approaches. At least since the 1940's, they have not looked to the proletariat as the only group capable of acting on their message. Indeed, Critical

[2] Ibid., p. 207.

Theory began largely as a reaction to disappointment in the political development of the European working classes. But neither is the proletariat excluded as a vehicle for social betterment. Critical Theorists seem to remain open to the possibility that almost any element of society might find occasion to act on critical insight, to break through the limitations of the present order. The one group implicitly discounted in this respect are established elites, those with the strongest stake in the present order. We therefore would not expect to see Critical Theorists participate in "problem solving" efforts as expert advisors. To accept elites' definitions of what is "problematic," and to work for change within the constraints of the present order, would go against the very nature of Critical Theory.

THE CRITIQUE OF INSTRUMENTALISM

To my mind, Critical Theory makes its most fruitful contribution in its critique of the role of scientific thought in modern, highly developed societies. Instead of helping people to enhance the human potential of their lives, bureaucratized research has turned into a monster of repression. Science and technology have "run wild." They have become devoted to streamlining the attainment of the ends of the powerful, yet never serve to examine or criticize those ends. The result is sophisticated technological manipulation leading to such anti-human prospects as environmental disarray, mass propagandization, and nuclear destruction. Critical Theorists thus picture the crowning irony of modern industrial society as the endless refinement of rational, scientific means to increasingly irrational long-term ends.

The role of social science in all of this, according to the Critical Theorists, does not differ much from that of natural science. Instead of an enlightening force to overcome repression, social science tends to become another tool of irrational long-term ends. Examples might include the role of social science in propaganda, manipulative management techniques, or seductive merchandising. Worst of all, in this view, is the tendency of social science to become part of a manipulative *Weltanschaung*—a world view where people are seen only in terms of their potentials for serving others' foregone ends. Critical Theorists like to use terms like *instrumentalism* or *objectification* for such instances of what they regard as the treatment of people as things, rather than as ends in themselves.

Critical Theorists characterize this separation of technical from value rationality as a strictly historical phenomenon. Only since the end of the Enlightenment have theorists despaired of subjecting value questions to the same critical scrutiny as technical ones. As Max Horkheimer wrote:

> Kant reduced the concern with man to three questions: "What can I know? What ought I to do? What may I hope?" The third question, which is "at once practical and theoretical," includes the other two. Examination of this third question leads to the idea of the highest good and absolute justice. The moral conscience, upon the truth of which depends the difference between good and evil, rebels against the thought that the present state of reality is final and that undeserved misfortune and wrongdoing, open or hidden, and not the self-sacrificing deeds of men, are to have the last word.[3]

Identifying himself with Kant's affirmation, Horkheimer continues:

> Reality indeed does not seem able to promise fulfillment of man's claims on it, but this does not mean that the idea of the world "in so far as it may be in accordance with all ethical laws"—in other words, the idea of a just order of things— "may [not] have, and ought [not] to have, an influence on the world of sense, so as to bring it as far as possible into conformity with itself." Such is the consequence of man's autonomy.[4]

[3] *Critique of Instrumental Reason* (New York: Seabury Press, 1974), p. 2.
[4] Ibid., pp. 2–3.

Thus, the distinctive *attitude* of Critical Theory is clear enough. But we may well ask whether this characteristic attitude corresponds to a logically distinctive intellectual method. For the notion of systematically contrasting the disappointing realities of the present to "what could be" is hardly unique to Critical Theory. As Chapter Two noted, many left-oriented social critics have developed variants of this idea. Indeed, there is no reason why a similar position might not serve the purposes of conservative critics wishing to promote a return to the "good old days."

For that matter, Robert K. Merton, that eminent spokesman for the sociological center, interprets his view of the role of understanding in social betterment as an attack upon:

> . . . inadequacies or failures in a social system . . . such that the collective purposes and individual objectives of its members are less fully realized than they could be. . . .[5]

Critical Theorists would no doubt wax indignant that their approach could be compared to "positivistic" thinking such as Merton's. But can we really identify a difference *in principle* between Merton's approach and that of Critical Theory?

If there is such a difference, perhaps it lies in the standard by which existing social realities are evaluated. Writers like Parsons and Merton view "social problems" as departures from values presumably shared by virtually all members of society. It is difficult to be sure of their exact position on this, but most Critical Theorists would probably find such a formulation unacceptable. True to their Marxist heritage, they would probably hold that any specific social order might foster "bad" or "inhumane" values. Such values might serve the interests of repression, might represent "false consciousness," as some Marxists would have it. Critical Theorists would want to subject such values to enlightened scrutiny. Such examination would presumably aim at substituting for "bad" values some more enlightened principle.

[5] *Contemporary Social Problems* (3rd ed.; New York: Harcourt Brace Jovanovich, Inc., 1971), pp. 819–820.

But all of this raises very serious logical problems. For how are we to characterize the "higher standard" to which repressive or otherwise inadequate social conditions are contrasted? I believe that Critical Theorists are right to be skeptical of the approach favored by Parsons and Merton, that of contrasting existing reality with the values of society "as a whole." Such an approach risks confusing the values of dominant groups, or simply passive acquiescence to the *status quo*, with the moral sensibilities of all. But this "value consensus" assumption at least solves the problem of identifying some standard, other than the personal predilections of the investigator, for what constitutes "improvements" in social conditions. If Critical Theorists reject this approach, what alternative can they offer?

One other approach would be to judge every empirical social setting in relation to some absolute and unchanging set of values. To be sure, justifying any particular choice as superior to all the other possibilities would be no easy matter. True, if it could be done, it would solve the problem of defining what has been called an "Archimedean point" for social criticism. But Critical Theorists would almost certainly reject this possibility as well. For they would no doubt argue that a critique of established social relations proceeds, so to speak, stepwise. The role of reason, in other words, is not to judge all social reality according to the same standards, but rather to draw from every situation its unique potentials for social betterment. In Horkheimer's words:

> . . . in regard to the essential kind of change at which the critical theory aims, there can be no corresponding concrete perception of it until it actually comes about. If the proof of the pudding is in the eating, the eating here is still in the future.[6]

Most proponents of Critical Theory, I believe, would join Horkheimer in his unwillingness to give a closer characterization to the changes sought by their method. The remarks of his cited earlier

[6] *Critical Theory,* pp. 220–221.

in this chapter are the most explicit account of the aims of Critical Theory known to me.

DIFFICULTIES IN THE APPROACH

I have tried, in the preceding statements, to render the position of Critical Theory as much as possible in the terms its exponents would choose. But this is difficult, for I see these arguments as so ridden with logical confusion and sociological implausibility as to leave them very unconvincing. The proof of the pudding may well be in the eating, as Horkheimer assures us; but the satisfaction or dissatisfaction of the diner must be governed by *some* particular taste. It is fair enough to insist that the critique addressed by Critical Theory to any concrete situation must be specific to that situation. But proponents of the method must be able to offer some generalizations, however abstract, about the overall directions implied in such critiques. Failing this, the judgments of Critical Theorists inspire about as much confidence as those of the naïve art lover: All they know for sure is that they know what they like.

I do not mean to suggest that a solution to this quandary ought to be easy. On the contrary, it is perhaps the most perplexing riddle confronting the doctrines considered in this book; all the arguments about it seem to founder at one point or another. But spokesmen for Critical Theory do not even seem to take the questions seriously. As a result, their answers come out sounding like pretentious platitudes.

Such is the effect, in any case, of statements like Horkheimer's that "The moral conscience . . . rebels against the thought that the present state of reality is final and that undeserved misfortune and wrongdoing, open or hidden, and not the self-sacrificing deeds of men, are to have the last word." No doubt, most people indeed do prefer to see self-sacrifice prevail over undeserved misfortune and wrongdoing—though one wonders how meaningful statements in such general terms may be. But, as Weber would remind us, such preferences still provide no logical formula for refuting someone who perversely espoused an opposite preference.

More importantly, such sweeping pronouncements provide absolutely no clue to the *implementation* of such values in practice. Does "justice" in contemporary America require reverse discrimination, say, on behalf of women and blacks, to compensate for past injustice? Or must we exclude such measures as inherently unjust and hence unacceptable? Does "making a decision in favor of peace," as Habermas enjoins us to do, mean that the value of peace must always override the importance of redressing grave social inequities? Such questions are hardly farfetched; indeed, they make up the stock-in-trade of political discussion. Any program for furthering "rationality" in social relations which ignores the need for specific answers to such dilemmas clearly fails a major part of its task.

Such ambiguities leave us with no assurance that any two practitioners of Critical Theory would come up with similar recommendations for the "rational" improvement of specific social conditions. One thinks of Max Horkheimer's attack on the Pill as a cause of dehumanization in sexual life; made in the 1960's, his arguments scandalized the younger adherents of the movement. But who can say whether Horkheimer or his youthful critics were truer to their critical principles? Is carefree sex, with the possibility of casual promiscuity, more or less "dehumanized" than a sexual life in which every experience is tied to the possibility of conception? Does Critical Theory offer any way of settling such important practical questions—either through analysis of the concepts involved or through investigation of empirical social phenomena? If not, Critical Theory hardly advances the concerns of this book. Indeed, the doctrine seems to abandon the field of discussion just when the going gets tough.

CRITICAL THEORY AND SOCIAL CHANGE

But this is scarcely the end of the difficulties with Critical Theory. Perhaps more serious is its failure to explore seriously the *feasibility* of different forms of desired social change. Critical Theorists rarely give any detailed consideration to what concrete social rearrangements, if any, might be able to bring the better world which they seek into existence.

Antagonists of Critical Theory have often characterized its arguments as utopian. Exponents rejoin that this impression merely stems from the fact that they deal with possibilities for social change which are no more than latent in the present situation. Herbert Marcuse writes:

> In making this demand of the essence of man, [critical] theory points the way from the bad current state of humanity to a mankind that disposes of the goods available to it in such a way that they are distributed in accordance with the true needs of the community. Here men would themselves take on the planning and shaping of the social process of life and not leave it to the arbitrariness of competition and the blind necessity of reified economic relations. The power of the conditions of labor over life, along with the separation of the immediate producers from the means of labor, would be abolished. Instead of life being placed in the service of labor, labor would become a means of life. Instead of degrading cultural values to the rank of privilege and object of "leisure," men would really make them part of the common existence. These determinations of essence are distinguished from utopia in that theory can demonstrate the concrete roads to their realization and can adduce as evidence those attempts at realization which are already under way.[7]

Note how Marcuse, referring to the sweeping changes envisaged here, affirms that "theory can demonstrate the concrete roads to their realization." Yet one searches in vain, both in Marcuse's remarks and throughout the literature of Critical Theory, for a closely reasoned discussion of the feasibility of such plans. *How* would goods be distributed "in accordance with the true needs of the community?" What particular institutional arrangements

[7] *Negations* (Boston: Beacon Press, 1968), p. 73.

would put such distribution into effect? What grounds do we have for believing that popular sentiment would support these particular arrangements, as against the many other plausible possibilities? Such questions represent the fundamental ingredients of most political and social debate. Persuasive answers to them would certainly count as major contributions to social betterment. Yet, such discussions are not to be found in the writings of Critical Theorists. They seem to regard the sweeping proclamation of the values which they favor as tantamount to providing assurance that these values can be implemented.

Pressed with these criticisms, spokesmen for the method may simply deny their relevance. There is no point in *planning* for the implementation of any future, rational social order, they may insist. For such an order will arise directly from the enlightened wills of those concerned, rather than through the imposition of a manipulative plan from outside. "Positivistic" social science, it may be alleged, misleads us by judging the possibilities of a newer, better world by the standards of the inadequate present one.

Thus, Marcuse urges us to

> . . . risk defining freedom in such a way that people become conscious of and recognize it as something that is nowhere already in existence. And precisely because the so-called utopian possibilities are not at all utopian but rather the determinate socio-historical negation of what exists, a very real and very pragmatic opposition is required of us if we are to make ourselves and others conscious of these possibilities and the forces that hinder and deny them.[8]

He seems to take it as self-evident that "the determinate socio-historical negation of what exists" represents a potentially workable, complex social whole. The willingness of people to support these radically new institutional arrangements he seems to regard as beyond question.

Such assertions are at first obscurantist and finally anti-intellec-

[8] *Five Lectures* (Boston: Beacon Press, 1970), p. 69.

tual. Certainly, it is difficult to assess possibilities for new social forms on the basis of evidence drawn from qualitatively different social systems. But refusing to attempt such assessments hardly represents a satisfactory alternative. Anyone who fails to consider how specific institutional innovations may or may not serve the needs and desires of individuals in an "improved" social world runs the risk of founding institutions that work very inhumanely indeed. Not all instrumental thinking need be selfish.

When Critical Theorists talk of realizing potentials for social betterment, they tend to emphasize enhanced satisfaction of individual needs. "Improved" social relations, in their view, are those which allow for the full flowering of each person's true potential. We know that human life is capable of being so much more than it is, they seem to say; let us, therefore, demand a world which makes good these potentialities.

This impulse is unexceptionable—and, I might add, scarcely the exclusive property of Critical Theory. But one of the classical problems of social thought is that of how far specific social arrangements can go to allow for the fulfillment of each individual's needs. We certainly have no guarantee that any single set of institutions can provide for the equal fulfillment of *all* members of any society. We must recognize the very real possibility that, in some cases, one person's utopia would be another's purgatory. Social inquiry in the service of social betterment thus faces some very difficult tasks. It must attempt to envisage specific social arrangements which meet the needs and wishes of the largest possible numbers of people. Preferably these would be institutions which both offer the greatest possible measure of freedom to all and yet maintain some minimal coordination. Such conditions are almost platitudinous to affirm, yet endlessly difficult to strive for. Critical Theory does not provide much help.

I argued in Chapter Three that clashes of political doctrine are not wholly, and often not mainly, mere collisions of opposing value systems. Many of these contests actually turn on complex social scientific arguments about how social, political, and economic systems *work*—and on how they *might work* under changed conditions. Does progressive education help children to acquire basic skills as effectively as traditional education? Must socialist planning necessarily bog down in unwieldy over-bureaucratization? Are "failures" to achieve progressive social changes the result of a purposeful "system" of reactionary forces or the effect of mere constellations of accidental circumstances? These broad questions are extremely complicated and value-laden. They require not only study of existing and historical social settings, but also educated conjecture about human action under altered conditions in the future. At least they are empirical questions, ones to which conscientious research and study may, at best, contribute. Such questions are a staple of political discussion and of much practical social planning—though people may not recognize their sociological content as such. But Critical Theory does not contribute much to these important discussions.

HABERMAS: A NEW TACK

Many of the difficulties of Critical Theory as an approach to rational social betterment stem from the proletariat's absconding from its role in "classical" Marxism. Earlier Marxists could rest their faith in growing working-class political consciousness and strength. These forces, it was felt, represented the guarantors of a "better world"; whatever aided them helped the cause of social rationality. As Critical Theorists became more disenchanted about casting the Western working classes in this role, they had to seek another criterion for social amelioration. Thus, they developed ideas of "enlightenment" or "rationality" without specific reference to particular historical or social class groupings. Those tendencies from any quarter which promoted enlightenment or critical consciousness were thus to be encouraged. But the greatest difficulty with this approach, I have argued, is its failure to deal with

seriously Weber's dilemma. What guarantee can the Critical Theorists offer that others will share their standards of "enlightenment"? What standard, either logical or sociological, can yield
consensus over the meaning of rational improvement in social conditions? This difficulty clearly has much in common with problems
faced by more positivistic approaches to reasoned social amelioration.

Since the 1960's Jürgen Habermas, beginning within the tradition of Critical Theory, has attempted to deal with some of these
difficulties. Habermas has not been satisfied merely to deplore
Weber's conclusions on the dualism of fact and value. Instead, he
has brought together elements of linguistics, psychoanalysis, and
the history and philosophy of science in an attempt to build rational bases for resolving the clash in disparate political and social
perspectives. Many students of Critical Theory see this new departure as the most important intellectual development since its
beginning. The following pages aim to give a brief glimpse of what
he has in mind.

This, however, is not an easy task. Habermas's eclectic and
wide-ranging arguments would be difficult enough to summarize
if written by a master of lucid exposition. As it is, his writing
gives one the feeling of flying at very high elevations over a fog-
bound landscape; one can be certain only of the most prominent
peaks and contours. Naturally, his supporters attribute this effect
to the breadth of his vision and the profundity of his thought; his
detractors, as one might imagine, detect an underlying confusion.
Thus in the following remarks, wherever possible, I have tried to
let Habermas speak for himself.

Habermas fully endorses the insistence that scientific thinking
must yield conclusions on questions of ultimate value. Like the
Critical Theorists, he views the separation of value questions from
empirical ones as a strictly historical phenomenon. The modern
view, he contends, stems from a misguided equation of the methods and concerns of the natural sciences with those of all scientific

inquiry. Attempting to redress what he regards as a misconception, Habermas contrasts the logic of different forms of scientific inquiry as follows:

> The approach of the empirical-analytic sciences [the natural sciences] incorporates a *technical* cognitive interest; that of the historical-hermeneutic sciences incorporates a practical one; and the approach of critically oriented sciences incorporates the *emancipatory* cognitive interest that, as we saw, was at the root of traditional theories.[9]

This concern to link *ways of knowing* about the world with the nature of the underlying human *interest in knowing* is central to Habermas's argument. Here Habermas joins a very long tradition in German thought—that which emphasizes a deep distinction between *Naturwissenschaft* and *Geisteswissenschaft,* or the natural versus the cultural sciences. The motives underlying natural science inquiry are fundamentally different, he feels, from those underlying other forms of knowledge. His account of natural science goes as follows.

> Theories [in the natural sciences] comprise hypothetico-deductive connections of propositions, which permit the deduction of lawlike hypotheses with empirical content. The latter can be interpreted as statements about the covariance of observable events; given a set of initial conditions, they make predictions possible. . . .
> In controlled observation, which often takes the form of an experiment, we generate initial conditions and measure the results of operations carried out under these conditions. . . . We can say that facts and the relations between them are apprehended descriptively. But this way of talking must not conceal that as such the facts relevant to the empirical sciences are first constituted through an a priori organization of our experience in the behavioral system of instrumental action.[10]

[9] *Knowledge and Human Interests* (Boston: Beacon Press, 1971), p. 308.
[10] Ibid., pp. 308–309.

Summarizing the above discussion, he characterizes the interest underlying natural science as "the cognitive interest in technical control over objectified processes."[11]

Habermas means to establish a deep qualitative distinction between this form of interest and that which may, at best, inform social inquiry. He writes:

> The systematic *sciences of social action,* that is economics, sociology, and political science, have the goal, as do the empirical-analytic sciences, of producing nomological knowledge. A critical social science, however, will not remain satisfied with this. It is concerned with going beyond this goal to determine when theoretical statements grasp invariant regularities of social action as such and when they express ideologically frozen relations of dependence that can in principle be transformed. To the extent that this is the case, the *critique of ideology,* as well, moreover, as *psychoanalysis,* take into account that information about lawlike connections sets off a process of reflection in the consciousness of those whom the laws are about. Thus the level of unreflected consciousness, which is one of the initial conditions of such laws, can be transformed. . . .
>
> The methodological framework that determines the meaning of the validity of critical propositions of this category is established by the concept of *self-reflection.* The latter releases the subject from dependence on hypostatized powers. Self-reflection is determined by an emancipatory cognitive interest. Critically oriented sciences share this interest with philosophy.[12]

As almost always, Habermas's statement on these important points is vague and allusive. But he seems to be saying, in these three statements, something like the following: Natural science inquiry results from the shared human interest in *manipulation* or *control* over the non-human world. The "laws" of natural science simply reflect the efforts of the scientific community to codify results of

---

[11] Ibid., p. 309.
[12] Ibid., p. 310.

their efforts in this direction. Social science may also aim at uncovering laws resembling the laws of natural science. Such knowledge (he states elsewhere) may serve the interests of *control or manipulation of people,* as natural science serves the interest of control over things. But social science can also lead to *enlightenment* and *emancipation.* This it can do by pointing to areas where people share an interest in the amelioration of human relations, and where unrealized possibilities of such amelioration can be known to exist. This shared interest in the improvement of human relationships, and the reflective or critical thought processes which arise from it, represent a qualitatively different relationship between the knower and the thing known from that between the thinker and an object of manipulation. This latter relationship forms the basis for his version of Critical Theory.

Such, at least, seems to be Habermas's intent. But his statements raise many questions. What does Habermas really mean, for example, when he so sweepingly characterizes the interest underlying natural science as that in "technical control over objectified processes"? Presumably not that all natural science investigations are undertaken strictly as means to perfect some form of control over the environment. For many investigations in "pure science" entail no anticipation of practical application whatsoever. Nor can one hold that the *techniques* of natural science investigation invariably require manipulation of or even intervention in the natural world. Astronomers often cannot intervene, even experimentally, in the worlds they study; and geologists and paleontologists may study worlds so far in the past as to be permanently beyond the reach of human manipulation. Moreover, if we are to believe the experiential reports of scientists, pure science is subjectively worlds apart from technology. Many "pure" scientists describe the greatest rewards of their work as the inherent satisfaction of what Popper calls the "spiritual adventure" of intellectual life. These concerns do not seem to have anything to do with manipulation or control, either in the experimental sense or any other. Thus, it is unclear in what sense Habermas is using the term when he talks about natural science deriving from "a cognitive interest in objectified control."

Nor do the remarks quoted above fully clarify the difference between forms of thought aiming at what he terms control, on the one hand, and emancipation, on the other. Of course, the distinction may lie simply in the definitions of his terms—i.e., efforts to control non-human things versus efforts to control or modify social relations of which one is a part. But I believe that Habermas means to point to a more profound difference, one which nevertheless remains less than completely clear. True, natural science does often serve to help in shaping the non-human world more to our needs and liking—e.g., in the control of disease. But is the kind of thinking involved in research and technology aimed at disease control fundamentally different from that, say, involved in the improvement in medical or educational services?

One fails to detect a fundamental difference between the *forms of thought* employed for purposes of self-betterment and those figuring in destructive calculations. Research for germ warfare has been described as a sort of application of epidemiology in reverse. Brainwashing and similar forms of psychic manipulation, it has been argued, represent nothing more than brutal applications of principles which figure in psychotherapy. The critical analysis of one's own neuroses, or of the shortcomings of one's own society, would seem to proceed according to the same logical principles as if the conditions were those of another person or another society. Indeed, self-correcting or even self-improving processes exist even in non-human systems, such as the cybernetic systems used in radar. Habermas's treatment of this issue fails to distinguish the difference which he seems to consider central to his argument.

SOCIAL BETTERMENT THROUGH DISCOURSE

But these difficulties are small in comparison to those surrounding Habermas's formula for rational resolution of practical social disputes. Habermas believes that the "emancipatory cognitive interest" can fuel concerted efforts to raise the quality of social life. Moreover, he believes that people's self-reflective faculties provide a way to "rational" resolutions of social disputes which all participants could acknowledge as such. He does not advance this argument on the basis of empirical evidence, but theoretically, with reference to the logic of the cultural world that we share. He writes:

> The human interest in autonomy and responsibility is not mere fancy, for it can be apprehended a priori. What raises us out of nature is the only thing whose nature we can know: *language*. Through its structure, autonomy and responsibility are posited for us. Our first sentence expresses unequivocally the intention of universal and unconstrained consensus. Taken together, autonomy and responsibility constitute the only Idea the [sic] we possess a priori in the sense of the philosophical tradition. . . . Reason also means the will to reason. In self-reflection knowledge for the sake of knowledge attains congruence with the interest in autonomy and responsibility. The emancipatory cognitive interest aims at the pursuit of reflection as such. My . . . *thesis* is thus that *in the power of self-reflection, knowledge and interest are one.*[13]

So, something about our common participation in the world of language signifies a shared interest in realizing "emancipatory" principles, such as autonomy and responsibility. Elsewhere Habermas writes, to much this same point:

> The validity claim of norms is grounded not in the irrational volitional acts of the contracting parties, but in the rationally motivated recognition of norms, which may be questioned at any time. The cognitive component of norms is, thus, not limited to the propositional content of the normed behavioral expectations. The normative-validity claim is itself cognitive in the sense of the supposition (however conterfactual) that it could be discursively redeemed—that is, grounded in consensus of the participants through argumentation.[14]

[13] Ibid., p. 314.
[14] *Legitimation Crisis* (Boston: Beacon Press, 1975), p. 105.

Again, the meaning of these statements is not exactly transparent. Perhaps Habermas is saying that conceiving of any particular form of behavior as "correct" or "appropriate" implicitly raises the possibility that such appropriateness might be questioned. And this assumption, he seems to be saying, opens the way for serious dialogue among rational participants on the matter. It all has a faint ring of Durkheim's notion of the non-contractual bases of contract.

Unfortunately, Habermas's argument has little of the rigor of Durkheim's. Habermas's discussions of "emancipatory interests" raise all the same difficulties encountered by the Critical Theorists in specifying terms like "enlightenment" or "reason." It is trivially true to assert that people share an interest in making their world "better" or "more enlightened." But what guarantee do we have that the nature of "betterment" for one person is at all consistent with "betterment" for another? What guarantees that one person's "emancipation" may not be another's constraint? Without answers to these questions, Habermas's "emancipatory cognitive interest" plays the role of *deus ex machina* in his arguments; it exists only because he could not get along without it.

Nor is Habermas much more illuminating about what it means for "validity claims" of norms to be "redeemed," or about the role of language in all this. Obviously, he believes that something about our ability to use terms like "just" and "reasonable" with mutual comprehension guarantees an ultimate ability to agree on the meaning of just or reasonable social arrangements under particular conditions. On the face of it, the claim seems incredible. Spokesmen for capital may extol the importance of "a fair return on investments," while trades unionists demand "a fair day's pay for a fair day's work." But their use of the same term hardly seems to guarantee that they could, on purely rational grounds, arrive at a mutually satisfactory contract settlement. Habermas's defenders would likely claim that these remarks miss the intent of his position, and we must not reject this possibility out of hand. He might well have clarified his intent here, if only he could simply provide

and discuss one full, concrete example. But the elliptical exposition of his approach in these passages is bound to leave most of
us scratching our heads.

Psychoanalysis has played a major role in forming Habermas's
thinking on these matters. He regards certain disputes over social
practice as entailing "distorted communication," analogous to
neurotic disturbances in speech or conduct. Like personality disturbances, he seems to be saying, social distortions originate in
something like traumatic events which then become perpetuated in
repetitive patterns. These "historical repressions," such as violence, exploitation, ignorance, or the like, leave their legacy in the
form of continuing unsatisfactory, unenlightened social relations
in the present. Rational social inquiry must approach these distortions much as a psychoanalyst does a patient's symptoms. It should
help people to understand the distortions of their social relationships *as* distortions and help uncover the historical origins of these
distortions. The method of reason should thus help once again to
make such relations whole and normal. Habermas writes:

> But just as in the clinical situation, so in society, pathological
> compulsion itself is accompanied by the interest in its aboli-
> tion. Both the pathology of social institutions and that of in-
> dividual consciousness reside in the medium of language and
> of communicative action and assume the form of a structural
> deformation of communication. That is why for the social sys-
> tem, too, the interest inherent in the pressure of suffering is
> also immediately an interest in enlightenment; and reflection is
> the only possible dynamic through which it realizes itself.[15]

Habermas's interpretation of the psychoanalytic method would
strike many of Freud's followers as selective indeed, but that need
not concern us here. Much more important are the disturbing
parallels between Habermas's position and the technocratic thinking of the "social problem solvers." Any notion of "distortions"
in language or in social relations obviously implies some idea of

[15] *Knowledge and Human Interests,* p. 288.

what "healthy" or "undistorted" forms must be. Likewise, the idea of the "validity claims" of norms requires some distinction between just or authentic norms, on the one hand, and unjust or misguided ones, on the other. Technocratic thinkers, I have argued, generate all sorts of confusions when they base their arguments on notions of social "health." They never succeed in developing a concept of "healthy" or "functionally integrated" social systems independent of their own partisan preferences. And Habermas seems to offer no argument which could resolve these difficulties where the others have failed.

Again, Habermas and his followers would no doubt contest any association between their method and the technocratic approach. Perhaps they would counter that Habermas's approach, unlike the other, does not regard the ends of rational discourse as foregone. Whereas the technocratic method regards social troubles or disputes as differences over means to ends which are essentially known, it might be said, the ends of critical discourse are *emergent*. That is, the outcome of truly rational deliberation cannot be known until it manifests itself through the conclusions of the participants. Such an interpretation of Habermas's position would at least strike a consistent line with statements like Horkheimer's that "the proof of the pudding is in the eating."

But the same objections raised in relation to Horkheimer's positions would apply *a fortiori* here. No matter how much one may regard the results of discourse as "emergent," one must have some criterion for distinguishing successful from unsuccessful emergences. How, in practical terms, is one to distinguish between successful "enlightened consensus" and some sort of inauthentic consensus, where parties may agree, yet where their new relationships are still not fully "rational"? Could such criteria ever be clear enough for all informed observers to come up with similar appraisals of outcomes of the method? Lacking a fuller and clearer account of these issues, we must regard them as unresolved.

As things stand, even Habermas's supporters show little unanimity about the exact intent of his argument at points like these.

One sometimes hears the interpretation that his discursive method does not really aim to *guarantee* that consensus on contentious social questions can be achieved in any specific case. In this view, Habermas's rational discourse simply provides the *best chance* for "rational" solutions, ones which do not slight the needs or concerns of any participant. This interpretation views Habermas's method as the ultimate anti-technocratic approach—one with absolutely no foregone aim of "solving" a "problem" by any particular standards.

But other passages make it clear that, with certain vague reservations, Habermas does intend his method to *work* to produce consensus. For example,

> What *rationally motivated recognition* of the validity claim of a norm of action means follows from the discursive procedures of motivation. Discourse can be understood as that form of communication that is removed from contexts of experience and action and whose structure assures us: that the bracketed validity claims of assertions, recommendations, or warnings are the exclusive object of discussion; that participants, themes and contributions are not restricted except with reference to the goal of testing the validity of the claims in question; that no force except that of the better argument is exercised; and that, as a result, all motives except that of the cooperative search for truth are excluded. If under these conditions a consensus about the recommendation to accept a norm arises argumentatively, that is, on the basis of hypothetically proposed, alternative justifications, then this consensus expresses a "rational will." Since all those affected have, in principle, at least the chance to participate in the practical deliberation, the "rationality" of the discursively formed will consist in the fact that the reciprocal behavioral expectations raised to normative status afford validity to a *common* interest ascertained *without deception*.[16]

Obviously, the conditions described here never meet with complete fulfillment in any real situation. Habermas means the "ideal speech situation" to be a heuristic extreme rather than an empir-

[16] *Legitimation Crisis,* pp. 107–108.

ical reality. But this passage makes it clear that Habermas intends his ideas to serve in real arguments to draw participants toward real, workable, "rational" conclusions.

Still, this passage raises more difficulties than it resolves. For if Habermas intends his discursive method as a practical measure for resolution of concrete clashes of interest, we must ask how broadly it is supposed to apply. Is Habermas telling us that discourse can resolve even those clashes which entail nothing more rational than zero-sum conflicts over the allocation of limited resources? Could the method, for example, point to a solution which both labor and management could accept as "rational" for distributing available resources between profits and wages? How do we distinguish between those disputes which turn on "generalizable interests" and hence presumably admit of "rational" solution, and those which do not? What proportion of the troublesome conflicts which social scientists might most like to address are susceptible to such solutions? And do we have any guarantee that different proponents of Habermas's approach would necessarily make similar diagnoses of these situations?

The only point where I have been able to find anything like a direct response to these questions is in a reply by Habermas to his critics, written in 1973. There he cites a comment by R. Bubner which seems so fundamental as to be nearly obvious:

> What characterizes an interest is, on the one hand, particularity and, on the other, *partial irrationality.* . . . In general, it is characteristic of interests that they compete with each other in a way that makes it impossible, on this level, to decide between them on the basis of real reasons. That is why the critical reflexion of the limitedness and inadequacy of empirically given interests cannot simply invoke another interest.[17]

Habermas's response to this very apt remark strikes me as vague and equivocal. He writes:

[17] "A Postscript to *Knowledge and Human Interests,*" *Philosophy of the Social Sciences* (June, 1973), Vol. III, No. 2, p. 177.

. . . practical discourses are capable of testing which norms manifest generalizable interests and which are merely based on particular interests (these can at best be subjected to a compromise, provided power is distributed equally).[18]

A response like this threatens to reduce Habermas's position to banality. A skeptical rendition of his argument might go as follows:

Sometimes participants in social conflicts may, by serious examination of one another's positions and of the nature of their differences, discover bases for agreement which they had previously neglected. For example, labor and management may, on consideration, decide to forego both profits and higher wages in favor of capital investment to increase both of these in the longer run. Such a rational consensus is a good thing, provided of course that the parties really have had a chance to study the situation freely, thoroughly and without coercion. Elsewhere, however, no basis for such a rational solution is possible. If not, the parties may simply arrive at a compromise somewhere more or less midway between their extreme demands, if their power relations are equal. Or if they are unequal, then they will arrive at a one-sided or exploitative solution.

All of this is virtually unexceptionable, but not very remarkable. It hardly represents a qualitatively distinct approach to social conflict resolution.

Lewis Coser has remarked that these ideas of Habermas's bear uncomfortable similarities to some otherwise very different doctrines. These are certain ideas of the "Human Relations School of Management." Proponents of this doctrine preached that labor and management could resolve their differences if only they could *understand* one another's problems and positions better. In this view, disagreement represented a simple and direct function of ignorance.

Although this doctrine had considerable influence in manage-

18 Ibid.

ment studies for a time, critics now generally regard it as naïve. Where conflicts of interest inhere in the structure of a situation, as often is true in industrial relations, parties do not necessarily become more agreeable by understanding one another better. In such instances, increased communication and better understanding may more likely sharpen conflicts than mute them. Many social conflicts, after all, stem not from "irrational" antagonisms based on misunderstanding but from authentic divisions of interest like the choice between profits and wages.

Habermas must respond to all of these issues. Ignorance of or lack of attention to potentially contentious issues may in fact confer stability and ensure peace. Thoroughgoing discussion, in which such things as habits of acquiescence, custom and power relations are ignored, may have the opposite effect. Perhaps the only certain result, if all social relations were indeed subjected to "rational discussion" by their participants, would be the outbreak of conflict and controversy in the place of apathy and acquiescence. This could mean strife and violence, both of which Habermas would surely deplore. Yet his program, as he presents it, provides no convincing assurance that such results could be avoided.

A more complimentary parallel than the one to the Human Relations School is that between Habermas's recommendations and the approach to value differences envisaged by W. G. Runciman. Runciman's good common-sense advice, as discussed in Chapter Three, went as follows:

> One tries . . . to secure the approval of one's interlocutor to the picture of the ideal society conjured up by the implementation of one's own political philosophy, and one tries to get him to accept that terms of approbation are more appropriate to one's own picture than to his. "But surely," one says, "it is more important that nobody willing to work should be allowed to remain unemployed than that extra entrepreneurial initiative should be rewarded by incentive payments," or whatever it may be.[19]

[19] *Social Science and Political Theory* (2nd ed., Cambridge: Cambridge University Press, 1969), p. 172.

But Runciman is less grandiose in his claims than Habermas, and to that extent more convincing. Runciman offers his strategy simply as a helpful gambit which may or may not work. Habermas actually seems to believe that something about participation in a world of normative culture actually *guarantees* that such clashes, or many such clashes, are soluble. But the concrete implications of his approach for the resolution of real disputes over specific social issues remain unclear.

To all of these criticisms, Habermas's proponents rejoin that they miss the true intent of his position. More extensive study of his writings, it is said, or of those which he cites, would resolve the apparent contradictions and clarify the seeming ambiguities. One hears these defenses offered both for Habermas and for others whose writings are both extensive and obscure. Such responses cannot be dismissed across the board; perhaps the way out of the wilderness really *does* lie just around the next turn in the road ahead. But the logical gaps in the writings cited above do not represent an auspicious sign. The questions which I have raised strike me as so obvious and so fundamental that any viable response would naturally be presented in these very discussions. And there is no reason why the author ought not to be able to offer such a response in straightforward language.

CONCLUSION

To Habermas's credit, he directs his efforts at perhaps the central problem in the Critical Theory tradition. Indeed, the question of how reason may attack clashes of interest and ultimate value is central to this book as a whole. We might view Habermas's attempt as an effort to create a sort of Critical philosopher's stone—a mechanism for converting the dross of everyday social antagonism and discord into the gold of enlightened consensus. The problem is so fundamental, and the project so daring, that success would clearly represent a milestone in social thought.

But Habermas's method, like the philosopher's stone, is slow to disclose its secrets.

Habermas's thinking in these directions is still very much in the process of unfolding. Those working within this idiom will no doubt continue to accord Habermas the benefit of the doubt as the process continues, even while disagreeing on his exact intent. The rest of us must inevitably remain more reserved. We can simply take note of the ambiguities discussed above and hope that further writings from Habermas and his followers may clarify them. Perhaps our attitude should be more like that to someone's claim to have perfected a perpetual motion machine than like that toward the notion of a philosopher's stone. We must withhold our praise until we can examine a working model.

Clearly the insights of Critical Theory, including those of Habermas, have enriched the discussions of this book. But their greatest contributions lie in the identification of problems, rather than in the provision of solutions. Critical Theorists are right to remind us that most people share a reaction against oppression, suffering, ignorance, destruction, and strife. But they do not really succeed in what Weber considered the impossible task of finding *logical* grounds for judging the value problems posed in the confrontation with such conditions. Perhaps even more seriously for our purposes, they offer very little help in deciding how to shape concrete social arrangements so as better to implement "enlightened" principles. Yet these questions provide the most nettlesome challenge to the role of reason in social betterment.

The difficulties faced by these writers are instructive. For they parallel the problems faced by other doctrines studied in this book as they attempt to identify an "Archimedean point" for social criticism aimed at social betterment. Despite the most earnest attempts, it has proven very difficult for any thinker to develop a program of "rational enlightenment" that does not ring suspiciously of the partisan preferences of the thinker himself. For the writers discussed in this chapter, the failure of the proletariat to act out its appointed role as "historical agent of rationality" has sharpened this dilemma. Deprived, ultimately, of faith in a single class, these writers have appealed to more abstract principles of "emancipatory interests," "liberation," and the like. Yet, the ambiguity as to what these notions imply as a program for enhanced insight in the service of social betterment has been only too apparent.

Habermas and the Critical Theorists remind us, and rightly so, that war, organized hatred, and the like represent dehumanizing frustrations to the best potentials of social life. But they do not point the way to alternate social arrangements which all concerned could acknowledge as just. Still less do they suggest how the study of empirical social reality might disclose possibilities for more satisfactory social arrangements. In their lack of effective attention to concrete institutional problems, they assume a pose which is not only unhelpful but also virtually anti-sociological.

6

Gunnar Myrdal: Making Beliefs and Actions "More Rational"

Nearly everyone, it seems, would like to see social processes work "more rationally." Most people also believe that the study of social relations can and should conduce to this end. But what does rationality entail, and how can we expect increased understanding to lead us in that direction? Here we find no unanimity, but a bristling bouquet of contradictory responses.

The difficulty, we have seen, stems largely from the partisan nature of the conditions we strive to address. On the one hand, the essence of a "rational approach" would seemingly be to transcend short-term conflicts in the interest of reaching some "common good" or "higher goals." But close examination of troubled social conditions shows that their very troublesomeness arises from opposition of interest and value among the parties concerned. We can hardly imagine any "solution" to problems such as pollution, racism, or poverty which does not favor some interests at the expense of others. Still less have we a guarantee that added understanding would necessarily help those concerned to adjudicate their differences more gracefully. What role can the social analyst take in transcending such troubled situations? Can he or she find a logically distinct position on behalf of "society as a whole?" And has anyone put forward a plausible rationale for how social inquiry might help realize such a position?

Gunnar Myrdal, the Swedish economist and sociologist, has contributed at least as much as any contemporary figure on this issue. The diversity of his accomplishments adds weight to these contributions. His work includes trenchant theoretical analysis, varied and acclaimed empirical research, and practical experience in the application of social research in social policy. In all of these works, he brings at least as much sophistication as anyone to the quest for a fair and impartial role for the investigator in instilling "rationality" in social relations.

POLITICS AND SCIENTIFIC JUDGMENT

Myrdal's opening contribution to these concerns was *The Political Element in the Development of Economic Theory,* first published in 1929. A work of historical erudition and analytical skill, it criticizes several major currents in economic thought since the earliest days of the discipline. Myrdal's target throughout the book is the concealment of partisan doctrines in the Trojan Horse of dispassionate scientific analysis. Most economic theorists, he observes, have paid lip service to Hume's idea that analysis of empirical fact can never lead to normative conclusions. They have held that the subject matter of economics is strictly factual—the study of verifiable empirical data and demonstrable cause-effect relations. Nevertheless, Myrdal argues, exponents of these doctrines typically end up offering conclusions about how political, social, and economic affairs *ought* to be conducted.

Myrdal is at his best in identifying the point at which partisan assumptions enter into "purely scientific" thinking. He writes:

> From a scientific point of view, nearly all our terms are . . .
> "value-laden." . . .
>
>   . . . These are teleological figures of speech, by themselves
> just as innocent as those which adorn primers of biology in
> which it is explained that the function of the heart is to act as
> the pump of the blood-system. But in economics it is, as we
> know, so fatally easy to proceed as follows: "As a reward for
> performing this function, he receives a profit," and thereafter
> to go further and regard the fact that the entrepreneur fulfills a
> "function" as constituting some kind of justification for the
> profit he receives.[1]

The trouble with these sorts of lapses, Myrdal argues, is that
they lead the unsuspecting reader to accept partisan political conclusions as inherent in "the facts" or "the nature of things." In
reality, analysis of "the facts" alone can never yield judgments
such as whether given rates of profit are reasonable, or indeed,
whether profit making is socially desirable. Such decisions turn
instead on value assumptions not susceptible to empirical verification.

Myrdal particularly attacks those who posit some objective notion of the joint welfare of all of a society. In a later book, he re-
capitulated this argument as follows:

> The idea that there is such a thing as a "common welfare," an
> "interest of society," which can be known, has followed us up
> to present times. It is seldom discussed but rather taken for
> granted. . . . The availability of this concept makes it easy
> and natural for the economist, and also for other social scien-
> tists, to apply a concealed valuation, covered only by this vague
> phrase, directly to his material or factual data. Statements that
> something is, or is not, desirable from the viewpoint of "so-
> ciety" will surprisingly often appear even in statistical work
> without any conclusive argument about how such a value judg-
> ment has been reached and precisely what it means.[2]

[1] *The Political Element in the Development of Economic Theory* (English ed.; London: Routledge & Kegan Paul, 1953), p. 20.
[2] *An American Dilemma* (New York: Harper & Brothers, Publishers,
1944), pp. 1046–1047.

Perhaps the most common manifestation of such assumptions is the utilitarian idea that the "general welfare" of society can somehow be calculated by summing the individual "utilities" of its members. The problem with such judgments, Myrdal notes, is that summation of different individuals' satisfactions requires value judgments. Whether a society is "better off" if ninety-five percent of its members enjoy a windfall of ecstasy, at the price of agony for the remaining five percent, is not a question that can be answered arithmetically. The goal is not to avoid such value judgments, Myrdal argues, for they are unavoidable in any political discussion. But he regards the idea that science can provide formulae for such judgments, acceptable to all reasonable observers, as illusory and dangerous.

Note the similarities between the fallacies attacked by Myrdal and functionalist views of society put forward by writers such as Durkheim and Merton. The latter picture social life as like a machine or a living system; "disorder" consists of flawed tuning of the constituent parts, such that one or more element does not play its proper role. The influence of this model has been extremely far-reaching, for it implies a clear-cut activist role for the student of society. The social scientist, as a specialist in the "natural" or "correct" relations of social elements to one another, can instigate disinterested intervention to restore flawed conditions to their "healthy" or "natural" state.

The notion that one can objectively identify a "healthy" state of society, of course, is simply another manifestation of the economists' notion of "common welfare" or "interest of society." Both represent intellectual sleight-of-hand, in which partisan political values take on the air of scientific verities. The alternative is to assume, with Myrdal, that any suggestions for "social improvements" require value judgments, choices among contending political interests that are not to be reached through analysis of evidence alone. And this conclusion places the burden squarely on the investigator as to what changes to seek, and how analysis may lead to such ends.

VALUATION AND BELIEF

How, then, does Myrdal resolve these issues in his own right? Can he both acknowledge the political element of all social thought and offer a perspective for the betterment of "social life as a whole"?

Key concepts in all of Myrdal's writings are *valuation* and *belief*. Valuations are ideas, usually shaped by people's social experiences, of what is desirable or worth striving for. Beliefs are empirical ideas about facts and causal relations—notions of what the world is like and how it works. His idea of valuations is, of course, much the same as Weber's idea of ultimate social values, but Myrdal adds an important assumption that Weber does not explicitly make. Valuations may not be "provable" in any tightly logical sense, Myrdal argues, but they are not wholly independent of empirical beliefs, either. Instead, people tend to arrange beliefs to support their valuations and attempt to shape their valuations to be consistent with their beliefs. Myrdal writes:

> In our civilization people want to be rational and objective in their beliefs. We have faith in science and are, in principle, prepared to change our beliefs according to its results. People also want to have "reasons" for the valuations they hold, and they usually express only those valuations for which they think they have "reasons". . . . With the help of certain beliefs about reality, valuations are posited as parts of a general value order from which they are taken to be logical inferences.[3]

From here, Myrdal goes on to argue that people's beliefs are not straightforward reflections of the world around them, and still less "scientific" interpretations of that world. Rather, he sees beliefs as opportunistically arranged to support valuations and vested interests. The desire to appear rational or reasonable, both to oneself and to others, causes us to seek out those data that strike us as most intellectually congenial and to close our eyes to discordant informa-

[3] Ibid., p. 1027.

tion. As Myrdal puts it, "All ignorance, like all knowledge, tends thus to be opportunist."[4]

This selective, dialectical relationship between beliefs and valuations provides Myrdal with the stepping-off point for his formula for the beneficial effects of social inquiry. The social scientist, according to Myrdal, is especially well suited to identify these selective perceptions of the social world as such and, perhaps more important, to generate accurate, pertinent information in their place. Thus, he writes:

> By increasing true knowledge and purging opportunistic, false beliefs in this way, social science lays the groundwork for an ever more effective education: making people's beliefs more rational, forcing valuations out in the open, and making it more difficult to retain valuations on the lower level opposing those on the higher level.[5]

Throughout his extensive writings, this formula remains central to Myrdal's view of the role of social inquiry. He consistently portrays social science as an educative force, one which, by changing people's beliefs, can make their valuations and, ultimately, their actions more "rational." At the same time, he seems also to believe that, by providing a reliable basis for social beliefs, social science can resolve social conflicts manifest in contending belief systems.[6]

The formative experience in Myrdal's development of these ideas came in writing *An American Dilemma,* his classical study of relations between blacks and whites in America. One cannot read any portion of this book without noting the discrepancy, as Myrdal saw it, between what he termed "the American creed," or the "authentic valuations," of American society and the day-to-day practices that governed relations between the races. The various

---

[4] *Objectivity in Social Research* (New York: Pantheon Books, 1969), p. 19.

[5] Ibid., p. 41.

[6] See, for example, *An American Dilemma,* op. cit., pp. 1030–1031.

patterns of discrimination against blacks, he concluded, could only take place as exceptions to the more general principles of egalitarianism and liberty enshrined in Americans' valuations. Only ignorance and misinformation could permit the persistence of such patterns. And indeed, *An American Dilemma* is filled with accounts of erroneous beliefs, on the part both of blacks and of whites, that serve to make inegalitarian racial arrangements seem "reasonable." Examples are the suppression of evidence about the frequency of lynchings, or the persistent myth that both blacks and whites were actually satisfied with the status quo. It fell to the social scientist, Myrdal concluded, to confront such illusory beliefs with accurate ones, and thus to make it possible for "the American creed" to be realized in relations between the races. And this formula became the basis for Myrdal's more general ideas about the relations between social inquiry and social betterment.

If, as LaRochefoucauld had it, "Hypocrisy is the homage which vice renders to virtue," then rationalization must represent the complement of expediency to reason. Everyone has noticed how people cultivate beliefs whose only merit is to make their words and actions seem more reasonable. Yet, it does not necessarily follow that Myrdal's overall strategy for social inquiry is justified. For although vested interests and self-serving valuations clearly do evoke rationalizing, distorted beliefs, *it does not follow that changing or destroying the beliefs will necessarily change the valuations or the behavior.* Myrdal actually assumes relatively close causal relations between beliefs and valuations, on the one hand, and actions, on the other. At the very least, such assumptions are not justified *a priori*.

For the sake of contrast, consider the position of Pareto, the Italian economist and sociologist. For Pareto, much of human behavior consisted of responses to deeply felt, unconscious impulses. These impulses represented ends in themselves. Yet, people wished to represent the behavior stemming from the impulses as fulfilling some longer-term, nobler social end. Thus, Pareto argued, people developed elaborate, socially stamped accounts serving to explain their behavior "rationally." For the impulse of political activists to grab power—a favorite example of Pareto's—people adduce the highest patriotic motives. For instinctive prudishness, people cite the disapproval of the gods. For innate conservatism, people extol the virtues of ancient ways.

But such rationalizations, in Pareto's view, are far from being accurate explanations of people's conduct; he would have ridiculed the idea that attacking the rationalization could ever change the behavior. For the impulses behind the behavior are deep-rooted and abiding, while the rationalizations are transient after-thoughts.

No doubt, Myrdal's formula does hold true in certain situations. But as a general method for shaping values and social behavior, it is hardly convincing. The evidence that people simply reject information tending to upset cherished prejudices and vested interests is simply overwhelming—both in social psychological research and from everyday life.[7] Anyone who has ever put off a dentist's appointment because of "other commitments," then put it off again even in the absence of such commitments, realizes that removing the basis for a rationalization does not always change the behavior being rationalized.

VALUATIONS AND RESEARCH STRATEGY

Myrdal's rejection in *The Political Element* of purely objective solutions to social policy questions obviously throws the choice of value perspectives squarely upon the investigator. How does he propose to choose? Myrdal holds that decision particularly important, in that it shapes the entire intellectual orientation of research, as well as its likely social impact. "All social study . . ." he writes

---

[7] See, for example, E. E. Jones and Jane Aneshansel, "The Learning and Utilization of Contravaluant Material," *Journal of Abnormal and Social Psychology*, LIII, 27–33. Also, Amitai Etzioni, "Human Beings Are Not Very Easy To Change After All," *Saturday Review* (June 3, 1972).

in *Asian Drama,* "is policy-directed, in the sense that it assumes a particular direction of social change to be desirable."[8] ". . . the value premises used in the study . . ." he continues a few sentences later, "[steer] the interests and [determine] the approaches, the statement of problems, and the definition of concepts."[9]

The implication that a single analytical apparatus can be relevant to only one value perspective may be overdrawn. Intellectual controversy, after all, may drive investigators with opposite political predispositions to apply similar analyses to similar data, in hopes that the results will bear out their position.[10] Were this never so, hopes for settlement of politically charged intellectual issues would be slender indeed.

Nevertheless, no one can deny that the values of the investigator play a vastly influential role in shaping social inquiry. How would Myrdal have us choose our value perspectives in these circumstances? His answer is that the investigator ought to adopt the values of those under study as the basis for the investigation. He writes,

> A value premise should not be chosen arbitrarily; it must be relevant and significant in relation to the society in which we live. It can, therefore, only be ascertained by an examination of what people actually desire.[11]

This formulation, one might note, represents a value choice in itself. There would be nothing logically inconsistent in taking the position that the investigator's own values ought to guide the study, regardless of whether they correspond to those of the subject population. Nevertheless, the characteristically liberal position that Myrdal takes would probably find much support.

Less widely congenial, perhaps, is his assumption that the value

[8] New York: Twentieth Century Fund, 1968, p. 49.
[9] Ibid.
[10] This is, of course, the central contention of Chapter Three of this book.
[11] *Value in Social Theory* (London: Routledge & Kegan Paul, 1958), p. 2.

premises of research ought also to correspond to those of people
who ". . . are influential in molding public policy."[12] Many ana-
lysts would make precisely the opposite assumption, i.e., that the
first problem is to arrive at a formula for defeating the influence of
those who presently hold power.[13] In his willingness to adjust his
program of research and intervention to the requirements of those
presently in power, Myrdal discloses something about his own political values.

But these misgivings are minor compared to the conceptual
problems raised by Myrdal's position. For the very idea of a single
set of valuations embodying the "will" of a particular society, "as-
certained by an examination of what people actually desire," in
Myrdal's words, can be problematic. Can we really be sure that
such unambiguous directions exist? Actually, many contemporary
sociologists do base their theories on an assumption of relative consensus of values, but Myrdal is too subtle for that. He realizes that
any society embodies various and antipathetic value positions, with
potentially contrary bearings on the conduct of research:

> A . . . fundamental difficulty springs from the fact that
> valuations are *conflicting*. Conflicts rage not only between in-
> dividuals and groups but also within individuals. People do
> not have uncomplicated, homogeneous, and consistent valua-
> tions. . . .[14]

How, then, to choose among them? Myrdal proposes to do so by
drawing a distinction among different kinds of values:

> In our civilization people ordinarily agree that, as an ab-
> stract proposition, the more general valuations—felt to be valid
> in relation to the whole nation or even to all human beings—
> are morally *"higher"* than those relating to particular individ-

[12] *Asian Drama*, p. 49.
[13] See, for example, Paul Streeten, "Introduction" in Gunnar Myrdal,
Value in Social Theory, p. xliv.
[14] *Objectivity in Social Research*, p. 67.

uals or groups. This is not an *a priori* assumption but a generalization founded on empirical observation.[15]

And he continues:

> We are imperfect beings, and it is most often the higher valua-
> tions that are pushed into the shadows in everyday living.
> They are preserved for expression on occasions that are more
> ceremonial in nature or that in one way or another are isolated
> from daily life where the *"lower"* valuations more often pre-
> dominate.[16]

Myrdal's program, quite simply, is to base research upon, and to
attempt to buttress, the "higher" valuations at the expense of the
"lower." He feels that the former will prevail, if only social research can point up the contradictions between them and the day-
to-day actions based on the "lower" values. This is the meaning of
his recommendation, quoted above, in favor of ". . . making it
more difficult to retain valuations on the lower level opposing those
on the higher level."[17]

Is this a reasonable program? A Pareto would obviously greet it
with derision, and I find it difficult to be much more sympathetic.
It would be much more plausible to argue that "higher" valuations
are "pushed into the shadows in everyday living" simply because
they have so little to do with the concrete forces shaping social
behavior. Myrdal characterizes "lower" valuations as opportunistic
and self-serving, implicitly suggesting that the "higher" ones are
"better," or of greater ultimate import. But the "lower" valuations,
such as the belief in the inferiority of blacks in segregated America, at least represent a guide to everyday social practice. "Higher"
valuations, such as "equal justice and liberty for all" or the like
would appear more "opportunistic," in that they serve to inflate
people's self-esteem on ceremonial occasions, without actually
shaping behavior in the crunch.

[15] Ibid., p. 16.
[16] Ibid., p. 17.
[17] Ibid., p. 41.

Nor is it necessarily clear that the valuations people apply to larger categories of people are necessarily "higher"—if, indeed, that term can be used without itself requiring a value judgment. Many people, after all, follow much more stringent standards of conduct in dealing with their intimate associates than they would expect to be followed throughout all of society. One reproves one's friends for behavior that would be no more than normal among most people. Who is to say that such cases are less important than those Myrdal has in mind, where people profess lofty abstract principles but act ignobly in the day-to-day?

Nor is this the end of the conceptual difficulties in Myrdal's scheme. For there are other ambiguous cases where different valuations seem to point in opposing directions, yet where one set of valuations does not seem "best" by any of the above rules. A case in point might be the clash of modern versus traditionalist values in a modernizing society, an instance discussed by Myrdal in *Asian Drama*. Myrdal writes:

> To a scientist engaged in making society more rational, it must be questioned whether he should not want to use the valuations people *would have* if their beliefs were *correct* and not distorted. . . .
>
> Moreover, valuations to be used as value premises should most often refer to a *future* situation. Particularly in broader issues, this situation may be far off. It might represent the results of great changes on all sorts of levels and even in the institutional structure of society.[18]

In other words, the investigator should try to imagine how people *would* think and act, if only they had full access to all the facts. And since the investigator aims to promote social change, one should try to imagine people's attitudes once the change processes have run their course. People's valuations under these hypothetical future conditions should then form the basis for social science investigation and intervention.

[18] Ibid., p. 66.

Now surely this formulation shows how badly things can go wrong when even the most sophisticated thinker pursues poor assumptions to their logical conclusions. Predicting changes of attitudes, even under well-controlled laboratory conditions, is hardly a rigorous discipline. To anticipate fundamental changes in the value orientations of entire societies, under conditions of sweeping social change, over long periods of time—this amounts to sociological alchemy.

How far in advance is the thinker supposed to look in anticipating the future value dispositions of those under study? Five years? Twenty? One hundred? And what sorts of cognitive changes can we assume in imagining "the valuations people *would have* if their beliefs were correct and not distorted"? What sorts of truths, in this *gedanken* experiment, are we to administer? Consider a hypothetical example in contemporary America. If one were to bombard the white Americans with proof that black children are consistently worse nourished and worse educated than their white counterparts, the attitudes of the white public would probably become perceptibly more favorable to government measures of assistance to blacks. If, on the other hand, one were to saturate the white public with information that blacks have generally higher rates of violent crime than do whites, one would no doubt see an effect in the opposite direction. Which outcome should we envisage in adjusting our research perspective to the valuations of those under study? It might be replied that one should try to imagine how people would feel if they possessed "all" of the "relevant information." But I cannot see how to interpret these terms without introducing one's own value judgments.

Myrdal acknowledges at one point that "To draw inferences about people's valuations in radically changed circumstances in the future is hazardous. . . ."[19] Actually, he understates the case; it is a utopian project. In practice, the attempt to put such a program

19 Ibid., pp. 66–67.

into effect would result in each investigator's positing the values which he feels people *ought* to have under conditions that he *would like* to see come about. This is probably pretty much what working social scientists do, anyway, but it hardly represents a concession to the actual wishes of those under study.

One wonders why Myrdal allows himself to pursue such an unpromising line of argument. The reason, I believe, is that it represents the only available solution to one of the central dilemmas of this book—the search for an intellectual viewpoint that transcends the status of the thinker's own partisan values and predilections. The search for such an "Archimedean point," to use Paul Streeten's term, has represented a stumbling block for all of the thinkers considered in this work. Myrdal's proposal to orient social inquiry to the values of those under study has the ring of democratic good sense and the effect, supposedly, of transferring the onus of responsibility from the investigator himself. The fact that this approach leads to muddles and contradictions in practice is difficult to face, since the alternative is to confront a thorny problem that does not easily admit of alternate solutions.

This is ironic. For this embarrassing, convoluted reasoning is analogous to the tortured arguments that Myrdal so deftly deflates in *The Political Element*. There he attacks doctrines holding that normative conclusions can somehow be derived from objective analysis of the facts. Yet in the arguments cited above, he attempts to do something very similar—to show how one can derive value assumptions to guide the study of a society without imposing one's own wishes upon those studied. In fact, of course, Myrdal does take quite partisan positions in the assumptions underlying his empirical research—*vide* his decision to orient his study of Asian poverty to the concerns of the established power holders rather than, say, those of militant revolutionary movements. But such choices, like one's predictions of social values under hypothetical and distant future conditions, are purely political. They can no more be directly derived from "facts" about present social reality than could the classical economists provide us with a value-free measure of "social utility."

Working social scientists, then, orient their studies to the values that they themselves consider "best"—at least "under prevailing circumstances." In practice, this means that they apply their own political judgments of what is good for the society in question. Myrdal proceeds this same way in his own empirical studies. There may be ways of making intelligent judgments among such political views, but the formulae of Myrdal's discussed above do not provide much help in this direction. Thus far, he has advanced only modestly beyond Weber's original position on the arbitrariness of ultimate values.

THE IMPLEMENTATION OF VALUES

Weber's best-known argument in this connection, the reader will recall, is his contention that sociological analysis cannot resolve clashes of ultimate value. Weber was also careful to point out, however, that analysis of facts and causal relations could indeed help people to act more rationally in the pursuit of their values and to understand better the value implications of alternate courses of action. As Weber stated,

> *If* you take such and such a stand, then, according to scientific experience, you have to use such and such a *means* in order to carry out your conviction practically. Now, these means are perhaps such that you believe you must reject them. Then you simply must choose between the end and the inevitable means. Does the end "justify" the means? Or does it not? The teacher can confront you with the necessity of this choice. He cannot do more. . . .[20]

Myrdal's position seems generally to parallel Weber's here. Myrdal seems to be emphasizing, in other words, that our views of

[20] H. H. Gerth and C. Wright Mills, *From Max Weber: Essays in Sociology* (New York: Oxford University Press, 1946), p. 151.

how the social world *works* have everything to do with how we wish to see our values implemented in practice. While *ultimate* values obviously play a key role in political consciousness, he seems to be saying, other important political values and principles are instrumental rather than ultimate. The latter, we assume, are rather abstract and very few; perhaps a good example would be "the equal worth of all citizens before the law" or "the right to entertain whatever political or philosophical views one wishes." On the other hand, institutions such as universal suffrage or the Bill of Rights represent means of implementing such values, and are presumably justified as instrumental values rather than as ultimate goods in their own right. At least, this is the most plausible account that one can give of this highly rationalistic view of institutions and social action.

Most social scientists nowadays would no doubt accept Weber's position that ultimate social values are not susceptible to proof through empirical inquiry. Either one believes that people ought to stand morally equal under the law, or one does not; the matter is hardly to be settled by evidence. But empirical evidence should bear on whether instrumental values do in fact promote what they are supposed to promote. One is free to accept or reject egalitarianism as an ultimate social good, for example. But one cannot reasonably claim to embrace egalitarianism as an ultimate value while proposing to implement such values through the hierarchical institutions of feudal society.

It is only in this sense, it seems to me, that one can speak about the "rationality" of people's social values at all. If Myrdal is to argue that a particular institution or practice, or the values or beliefs supporting them, are "irrational," he can logically do so only on the assumption that the values and practices in question badly serve some higher value. He is not explicit on these points, but this does seem to be the reasoning behind his arguments in *An American Dilemma,* for example. He seems to argue that segregated institutions, and indeed the values of segregated society, are

"irrational" because they do not serve the "higher" ends that
they are supposed to—namely, the egalitarian ultimate values of
the American creed.

Such a position is at least logically consistent. But we cannot conclude that it fits empirical reality without making some extremely
convenient assumptions. Unless we assume that the egalitarian
values embodied in Myrdal's highly abstract "American Creed"
really do represent the ultimate ends of most Americans, his view
of the educative or therapeutic functions of social inquiry col-
lapses. If we posit white supremacy or maximization of personal
advantage as the ultimate values of a majority of Americans, then
the racist practices that Myrdal personally deplores become no
more than "rational." If investigation demonstrates that people
love segregated institutions, not on the misguided premise that
they represent effective means to higher ends but simply as good
things in themselves, there would be little more to say.

Of course, there is not much danger of such a clear-cut disturbing finding arising from any specific factual evidence. Identification of ultimate ends of social action, and of the relations of specific institutions and practices to such ends, is an extraordinarily
interpretive business. In reality, positing such ends and explaining
such practices as means to them supposes a model of social action
which is simply excessively rational. Yet, the difficulties that result
if we reject this model are abundantly apparent. For doing so once
again leaves the whole question of what it means to establish "rational" social practices up for grabs.

PROGRAMS AND PROGNOSES

Myrdal's abstract strategies for the role of social inquiry in the
service of social betterment, then, leave many questions unanswered. But his greatest contribution to the concerns of this book
may lie not in those debatable formulas but in his critical analyses
and conceptual refinements. Most significant among these, it seems

to me, is his interpretation of social consciousness as interaction between *program* and *prognosis.*

These terms are introduced briefly in an Appendix to *An American Dilemma,* and receive little discussion as such elsewhere in Myrdal's writing. It is Myrdal's British collaborator, Paul Streeten, who has elaborated these ideas and accorded them the attention that they deserve. The following discussion draws on Streeten, then, as much as upon Myrdal himself.

Streeten explains the ideas of program and prognosis as follows:

> "Program" should be understood as a plan of intended action, e.g., a party program, the objectives of trade unions . . . etc. . . . It consists of certain objectives or ends, and rules about the manner in which these objectives are to be pursued.
>
> By "prognosis" is meant a forecast of the probable or possible course of events. A prognosis is based on observation and analysis, and consists of the application to particular instances of generalizations about the actual and hypothetical connections between facts and events.
>
> . . . "Prognosis" stresses the predictive character of analysis; "program" is a concrete formulation of policy.[21]

These insights may seem simple, but full appreciation of their implications could dispel much confusion. The Myrdal-Streeten model reminds us at once, for one thing, that political consciousness is not a simple emanation of ultimate values but a postulate of how valued ends may and may not be pursued in the real world. And this helps us to recall that every political action or position, crude or sophisticated, embodies a kernel of sociological analysis. What is the most promising response to the plight of the poor? How much should we expect coercion to mediate relations among nations? Answers to such questions, and all the others comprising the vast agenda of debate over public affairs, involve both value positions *and* empirical analyses of how the social world works.

[21] "Introduction" in *Value in Social Theory,* p. xiv.

One particularly valuable insight afforded by the Myrdal-Streeten model is the interrelatedness of disparate elements of political consciousness. People's programs depend on the prognoses that they entertain, and vice versa. "Programs without prognoses are idle wish-dreams or empty protests," Streeten writes.[22] And he adds, ". . . prognoses also depend upon, and are altered with, changing programs. Valuations depend on what changes we believe to be feasible. But the 'constants' which determine what is feasible may in turn be altered by people's valuations. Faith can move mountains."[23]

It is easy to agree that program and prognosis are attuned to one another; we notice the fact in every aspect of political and social life. As Streeten points out, conservatives tend to be skeptical about the possibility of fundamental changes in human nature and social institutions, while leftists tend to be optimistic on these scores. These correspondences are so finely tuned that one can often infer a great deal about a person's political views from a single fragment of his or her beliefs on some important subject. Like paleontologists reconstructing an animal in entirety from a single bone, one can often quickly visualize the whole from which the fragment derives.

The very idea of social consciousness as interaction between program and prognosis reminds us forcefully that a single political action can never be interpreted or evaluated strictly by itself, "on its own merits." For we derive the meaning of every political act from its role in some larger scheme of possibilities. Helping old ladies across the street may seem a good thing in itself, but if one has to ignore the occupants of a burning building to do so, the picture changes. Judgments about political action and social betterment are like that. They require us not just to evaluate the immediate "goodness" or "badness" of an action but also to assess all its consequences against those of any number of other actions one

22 Ibid., p. xvi.
23 Ibid., p. xxviii.

might have taken instead. Such choices among complicated alternate programs and prognoses are bound to be extremely complex.

This observation has some pessimistic implications for the role of reason in social betterment. It suggests, for example, that unalloyed considerations of "humanitarianism" or "decency" are never as straightforward as we would like to think. One might consider the provision of welfare relief to the destitute as an example of a step everyone could or should approve on such grounds. But an old-fashioned, Spencerian free-enterprise liberal would regard such a step as liable to cause more misery than it assuages, since it would sap the initiative of the poor and lead to proliferation of their misery in the long run. Similarly, a militant Marxist might oppose such welfare policies on grounds that, by taking the sting out of poverty, they postpone the ultimate revolutionary change that represents the only meaningful progress. One may reject the political calculations going into these two extreme positions. But one cannot deny that politics requires us to make calculations of this kind, and that prognoses do exist that make such seemingly severe programs reasonable.

The Myrdal-Streeten model also sharpens our appreciation of issues raised by the doctrines of such contrasting figures as Popper and the Critical Theorists. The former insists upon applying social insight in the form of small, incremental changes, as though each step could be evaluated solely "on its own merits." Yet it should be clear that such an assumption embodies what Myrdal and Streeten would term program and prognosis in its own right—and rather exacting ones, at that. Popper's position implies, for example, that drastic and fundamental social and economic rearrangements are bound to cause more suffering than they alleviate. Such a position is hardly justified *a priori,* but demands a reckoning of the likely costs of sweeping change against the equally undeniable costs of moderation. I have argued, in Chapter Four, that Popper does not provide justifications that would be required to make this case persuasive.

Exponents of Critical Theory often seem to suffer from the same difficulty in reverse. Their position has it that only efforts to change the structure of society as a whole will suffice to deal with the inadequacies of the present order. But this position fails to take seriously precisely what Popper insists upon with a vengeance: the need to evaluate the feasibility and results of every effort at change. The implicit assumption that such things will take care of themselves represents a prognosis in its own right—and, I have argued, a highly debatable one.

Even when people favor similar programs, they may find it hard to agree how to relate them to current events. Revolutionary socialists, for example, often argue bitterly over whether a particular event represents the beginning of the end of the capitalist regime or merely a temporary abrupt downturn in a longer period of gradual decay. Such debates, of course, can produce clashes as intense as those among proponents of utterly different political values. Even in instances where different parties have identical valuations and identical programs, differing prognoses—that is, differing analyses of the significance of events—can lead to serious disputes.

Finally, an absolutely fundamental fact of social and political life is that public controversy does not respect its participants' programs. Especially in a democracy, power holders rarely have the chance to move very far in implementing their own political programs before they come in for criticism from those entertaining other programs. This creates special difficulties for programs of far-reaching social transformation which entail painful rearrangements en route. The dislocations produced, say, in the changeover from a capitalist to a socialist economy will not be interpreted only in light of the socialist program that inspired them. Maliciously or ingenuously, those who do not accept the underlying program will interpret such difficulties in the light of other, more or less antagonistic programs. What are "temporary setbacks" for the "true believers" will represent for others incontrovertible evidence of the futility of the underlying political vision.

CHOICE AMONG PROGRAMS AND PROGNOSES

The divisiveness of debates over social and political matters, then, can be seen to arise from disparities of program and prognosis among the participants. Is there, then, any basis for rational choice among program-prognosis combinations? Can social science analysis, or any other approach, help to distinguish between good and bad, between reasonable and unreasonable programs and prognoses?

One answer to this question is, "Not necessarily." It is logically possible, under the Myrdal-Streeten model, for two people to entertain diametrically opposite programs even while embracing identical prognoses. People, in other words, may simply have opposing *wishes* about the direction of social change, despite similar views of how the social world works. Empirically, of course, such a thing is unlikely, since people most often tend to shape their prognoses to fit their programs, and vice versa. But to the extent that differences are purely ones of ultimate value, they do not stand to be adjudicated through empirical inquiry.

Nevertheless, prognoses are about the real world. They are social, political, and economic hypotheses in their own right. And surely, it would seem, thoughtful analysis of people's prognoses can help to distinguish between the good and the bad. Surely, for example, one can at least eliminate programs based on plainly unrealistic or irrational prognoses.

Consider the case of a millenarian religious sect. Cults spring up all the time with programs for conversion of the entire world, or at least the creation of a substantial following of faithful. The prognosis is that the world is hungering for their divine message, and that people need only hear the true word to be converted. Characteristically, such groups form around a charismatic leader, who manages to infuse his few followers with fanatical determination to make the program come true by acting on the prognosis.

One might be tempted to bracket such a program-prognosis

combination as purely irrational. What special reason is there for believing in *this particular* divine inspiration? How is the prognosis of this cult any more realistic than that of countless other extreme sects which spring up, collect a few followers, and then die off?

But the trouble is, although most millenarian movements are ephemeral, and quickly see their own prognoses invalidated and their programs blocked, a few do not. In some instances the movement succeeds and the program is fulfilled, even over-fulfilled. And such exceptions, while rare, are extremely important in their social and historical effects. The successful few—the cults that become the churches and political parties of tomorrow—are not necessarily identifiable through advance analyses of their prognoses. People's belief in a particular prognosis may in itself validate it. As Streeten points out, "Faith can move mountains."

Faith actually plays an important role in all sorts of secular political and social plans, as well. For every prognosis, every justification of the "reasonableness" of a particular vision of the social world, makes certain assumptions about the willingness of people to act "appropriately" within that framework. The Communist militant assumes, for example, that once workers realize that exploitation is abolished, they will no longer be inclined to strike. The proponent of laissez-faire capitalism assumes that, once the suffocating mechanisms of government control are dismantled, people will not want to form covert monopolies or labor unions. These programs can only succeed if people accept the rightness of the prognoses as matters of faith, as unquestioned assumptions in the formulation of their daily actions. And, as we have seen, political life seldom affords the proponents of programs the luxury of having them evaluated in terms of the prognoses that fostered them. Thus, Communist states must contend with the persistence of "bourgeois thinking" generations after the revolution. And free-enterprise systems find themselves short-circuited by the penchant of both capitalists and workers to shield themselves from the full force of open competition.

As Streeten implies in his discussion of program and prognosis, attempts to distinguish between more and less "rational" political visions on purely objective grounds are foredoomed. The success of programs depends enormously on people's faith in them and in their accompanying prognoses. And this faith does not always correspond closely with the quality of intellectual analysis embodied in them.

RATIONALITY AND FAITH

Does all this mean that social science has no help to offer in distinguishing among better and worse possibilities for social betterment? Does it mean that all schemes for social betterment are equally worthy, provided that people believe in them? Hardly. We need not take seriously, for example, proposals to manage the economy of a complex industrial society by means of barter, or notions of deciding every administrative and political question in such a society through participatory democracy. The unfeasibility of such programs, and the faultiness of the underlying prognoses, hold regardless of any popular determination to make them work.

The question is, then, how far can social scientific analysis take us in unraveling the points at contest among contending political visions? What proportion of all troublesome political clashes could we hope to mediate through destruction of erroneous empirical beliefs?

Myrdal modeled his views on this subject on his studies of race relations in America. In this field, sound research has destroyed a number of what we now regard as socially pernicious popular beliefs. Thanks to developments in psychological testing, for example, it is now impossible to maintain the existence of gross intelligence differences between blacks and whites. In current debates on this subject, those who posit any racial differences at all still see vastly more variation among individuals than between racial groups. Thus, even what is today regarded as a quasi-racist position on these matters would be considered astoundingly progressive by the standards of one hundred years ago.

So far, so good. But should this example provide hope that all troublesome social controversies will eventually give way to the solvent of specialized research?

A clearer answer might emerge here if we turned the question around. Can we imagine empirical questions about the workings of society, we might ask, authoritative answers to which would substantially narrow the range of debate on major political and social issues? What empirical questions, in other words, are central to the most important social and political controversies of our times? I would suggest that a list of such questions would prominently include the following:

> 1. What social forces account for people's willingness to work? Are the incentives of material need and status rewards essential to people's willingness to do their jobs, or would people perform their duties willingly without such inducements, if social institutions were properly arranged?
> 2. To what extent is people's propensity to commit crime a function of their view of the justice or injustice of the social system of which they are part?
> 3. What are the limits of decentralization and democratization of political decision making in complex societies? Given the maximum public determination to make democracy work, in other words, how far can institutional rearrangements go in the direction of leveling inequities of political power?
> 4. What is the absolute minimum of coercion necessary to maintain civil order within societies and peace among nations?

These questions are, of course, extremely broad. Nevertheless, I think every reader will recognize their importance and their centrality to present-day political discussion. Our assumptions about the answers to these questions—and without such assumptions, participation in political discussion is impossible—directly shape the positions we take on a vast array of much more specific issues. Or, to put it another way, if we had generally accepted, authoritative answers to such questions, the range of political debate would be sharply narrowed.

But there is an essential dissimilarity between questions like these and other politically relevant questions, such as that of racial differences in intelligence. That issue is susceptible to a specific research procedure—testing and analysis of resulting quantitative information. No single equivalent forum exists for the four questions cited above. The latter are much more diffuse. There seems to be no single critical experiment, no one specific form of data which one could expect to resolve these questions.

This is not to say that the questions are not empirical ones, nor to deny that data exist to bear on them. There are all sorts of relevant data, but they are not decisive. They have more the character of "clues" than of elements which, taken together, yield only one unambiguous answer.

Consider the first of the four questions, the one dealing with people's motivation to perform their jobs. It should be easy to recognize the implications of one's answer to this question for one's political world view. Those who believe that people can never be motivated to perform their jobs unless goaded by material want or seduced by status gratifications will generally, and not illogically, favor more hierarchical social systems. They will be skeptical about the possibility or desirability of easing the burden of those at the bottom of the social heap. On the other hand, those who feel that egalitarian social arrangements may actually stimulate people's motivation to work predictably embrace very different views. They are likely to support measures to take the sting out of poverty, or to back policies such as social security measures that affect all members of society more or less equally.

It is a measure of the empirical reference of questions like the four cited above that people readily cite factual arguments in responding to them. In debates over motivation to work, for example, conservatives are liable to cite cases of revolutionary societies whose leaders have had to reinstate material and status hierarchies after brief egalitarian experiments. Leftists are apt to note, in turn, cases like the kibbutz, where people seem to contribute their labors willingly without invidious hierarchies of reward. Each party will then, of course, advance ingenious arguments as to why the examples given by the antagonist are not germane. The latter arguments, of course, will be attacked in turn. And so it goes.

We have all participated in arguments like this. The problem with them is not that we lack pertinent information to bear on the questions. It is more the richness of rather fragmentary empirical evidence available to support any number of different positions. Each argument seems to represent an assemblage of discrete "clues" appropriate to support a single position rather than a decisive test whose result is persuasive to all. For an authoritative resolution of the question of work motivations, we would need something like a series of controlled experiments, using entire societies as units. One would have to vary systematically the rewards offered for employment under a variety of different conditions. Needless to say, any such program of inquiry is a utopian prospect.

Sociologists have often noted the array of untested empirical assumptions which must be made in the course of ordinary people's everyday lives.[24] One brews one's morning coffee on the implicit assumption that no one has substitued poison for the ingredients. One consults a physician on the assumption that the person really *is* a physician and not a steamfitter with bogus medical credentials. Any such assumption could be verified, but the verification of any great number of these assumptions would rapidly become a total preoccupation. So, we rely on circumstantial clues, the implicit rules of "reasonableness," which we instinctively sense but find hard to articulate. Only occasionally do the inadequacies of these rules of thumb defeat us. In fact, we have little choice but to rely

---

[24] Or, as de Tocqueville wrote, "If man were forced to demonstrate for himself all the truths of which he makes daily use, his task would never end. . . . He is reduced to take on trust a host of facts and opinions which he has not had either the time or the power to verify for himself, but which men of greater ability have found out, or which the crowd adopts." *Democracy in America,* vol. II (New York: Alfred A. Knopf, 1953), p. 8.

on them. Life must go on, and a few slender clues to the normality of the situation at hand are at least better than nothing.

We see much the same sorts of processes at work in reasoning and discussion about political and social questions—except that the "rules of normality" are more tenuous there. The most basic political discussion requires assumptions about highly complex and diffuse questions, such as the four cited above. We know that specialists can spend lifetimes exploring such questions, and yet remain in disagreement with one another. The evidence is so rich, and any conclusion involves the integration of so many disparate elements of evidence, that room for divergent interpretation often remains even in the most thorough inquiries. Yet, political life goes on, and we must often make assumptions about these questions on the slenderest of evidence. To reserve judgment would paralyze political thought as surely as our daily lives would be stymied by our checking every implicit assumption that we make.

On more discrete, researchable empirical questions, such as that of racial differences in intelligence, we can often note clear progress over time. Much less is this the case, however, when the questions are more diffuse, thematic ones, such as the four cited above. It is striking how similar the main features of the landscape of nineteenth century political debate are to those of today. The various alternative answers to the problem of people's motivation to work, as given by figures such as Marx, Comte, Spencer, and Bentham, would all have their exponents in the 1970's. Certainly the quality of debate would be improved; social science research has provided the partisans of all these positions with increasingly sophisticated arguments. One would like to think that the range of positions that can reasonably be taken has narrowed somewhat. But one could definitely not say that new insights have decisively resolved any of the basic, thematic antagonisms of the last century. We remain free to choose data to fit our prejudices or predilections, although the quality of data available for this purpose has distinctly improved.

Myrdal's central concern was to build a social science that would make itself socially useful by attacking *distorted* beliefs. But the various alternative responses to the thematic questions cited above do not necessarily embody distortions in Myrdal's sense. It is true that the pressures of one's own values and interests greatly shape one's selection of evidence as a basis for response to these questions. But the richness of available "clues" means that a variety of contrasting positions can be taken without overt distortion. One can reasonably believe in one's own position on many important questions like these without having to insist that one's antagonists are necessarily "irrational" in their ideas. Not all differences of view on these ambiguous but all-important questions, in other words, can be attributed to "distortion."

And again, one has no choice but to take one position or another on these questions. In the last fifteen years, three major public figures in America have been assassinated. Nearly every thoughtful person is aware of the disputes over the circumstances of each of these assassinations. The "official" version of each of the three events has it that the crime was the act of an isolated killer, without larger political significance. Each of these three official accounts has sophisticated antagonists as well as supporters, and the most thorough study of the evidence surrounding the cases has not generated consensus. The problem is not so much the absence of evidence as its susceptibility to different interpretations.

Probably most Americans have an opinion on the veracity of the official explanations, and perhaps on the various alternate theories. Neither the sophisticated nor the ignoramuses seem to have a monopoly on any interpretation. The remarkable thing is that what best predicts people's opinions on the assassinations is not the evidence that they have reviewed so much as their view of the larger political realities in America. For those who generally support the political center, it is difficult to imagine the sort of subterfuge necessary to fabricate the official findings. For those more antagonistic to entrenched powers and institutions, it is difficult *not* to believe in such fabrications. In the absence of more authoritative data than are now available, such predilections will continue to shape opinions.

Some day there may come to light, in one or more of these cases, decisive evidence that will illuminate the circumstances of the assassinations to the satisfaction of all. When this happens, many opinions will have to be revised. But the underlying views of American society giving rise to the disparate interpretations will not change that much, if precedent is any guide. For global interpretations change much more slowly than views on matters of discrete fact, even though the former may address strictly empirical issues. And it is upon such global assessments that we must all base our approaches to the complex decisions of political and social life.

All of this casts an ironic light on the role of social inquiry in the enhancement of "social rationality." A hard look at Myrdal's approach has suggested that research can indeed attack certain "irrational" social beliefs. But discussion has also pointed to the limits of rational criteria in criticizing the contextual assumptions that play a key role in all political and social controversy. Indeed, it would not go too far to suggest that a key determinant of one's positions on these matters is a measure of non-rational—though not necessarily *ir*rational—faith.

People often find themselves divided on how to approach even fairly delimited problems of "rational social action" because of differences in their over-arching political consciousness. No single event or issue or decision in political life, we have seen, is meaningful without some such context—without some program and prognosis, as Streeten or Myrdal might point out. Discussion of even such a mundane matter, say, as planning for hospital outpatient services or recreation facilities may turn on abstract considerations of the "best interests" of those concerned. And such questions, as we know, can open the whole Pandora's box of weighty and divisive issues.

Some of these sources of division are differences in the ultimate value affirmations of the participants. But elsewhere they may stem from differences on questions which are fundamentally empirical, but highly abstract and diffuse. Do the long-term interests of the working class lie more in a decisive break with the capitalist system, or more in a struggle to improve their position within that system? Can we expect crime and other "anti-social" behavior to disappear if major forms of social inequality are removed? There is at least a major empirical component to questions like these, and many fragments of evidence to bear on them. But the evidence alone does not absolutely constrain the selection of these fragments and their shaping into a coherent position. And this is where some article of faith must play a role.

All political positions embody such articles of faith. Some of these are much more vulnerable to closure through empirical inquiry than others. An article of faith among classical segregationists was the inherent inferiority of Negroes and the consequent inability of the latter to manage their own affairs. It is difficult to find an intellectually respectable defense of this position nowadays. On the other hand, a key article of faith among many pro-Soviet Marxists is that the present shortcomings of Soviet society are attributable to bourgeois vestiges, slowly but inevitably being overcome with passing time. Fundamentally empirical, this assumption is increasingly difficult to defend, but one could scarcely claim that it was without intelligent exponents. Another kind of faith is the moderate's belief that small, incremental changes are always preferable—safer, more effective, etc.—than the alternative. Faith in this assumption is widespread, and those who defend it include some of the West's most eminent thinkers. But there are all kinds of empirical grounds for questioning this sort of belief.

Such affirmations of faith, we have seen, shape people's approaches to even highly circumscribed questions of social action. If reasoned analysis of evidence could lead to decisive, unanimous choice among such positions, social inquiry would thereby contribute handsomely indeed to resolving the most troublesome questions of social life. But the trouble is, such closure is hardly likely.

Although the questions at issue are not metaphysical, the empirical issues involved are so diffuse and far-ranging as to resist resolution through any single breakthrough in empirical inquiry.

Sir Karl Popper notwithstanding, we cannot count on being able to deal with political and social issues in a piecemeal fashion. We often cannot solve small problems of planning and action without first addressing the big, contextual problems. And here, the contribution of reasoned inquiry is ambiguous. With the accumulation of social science findings, certain positions may slowly be abandoned or modified. Yet other debates show the greatest resistance to change through empirical evidence. Social science can narrow the range of positions which seem reasonable, and no doubt increase the quality of debate over such positions. But ultimately choice among such positions—with all the sweeping effects that this implies—must turn on at least some assumptions which are empirical in principle, but which remain highly resistant to resolution through debate on "the facts."

7

Can Understanding Help?

The ideas of this book run contrary to some of our deepest instincts in thinking about social change. Ordinarily we like to think about social processes in the same way that we think about "things." When some aspect of social life strikes us as unsatisfactory, our reaction is to seek out the malfunction and set it right. Thus, we think of social insight as having the same straightforward utility as understanding of the non-human world: If we know how social processes "work," we are in a position to have them "fixed" when they "go wrong."

By now, it is clear how much more complicated things are when one tries to assess the role of understanding in improving social conditions. True enough, social life offers plenty of conditions which we or others might regard as "malfunctions" of the social mechanism—intergroup conflict and hatred, racism, unplanned and disorderly social growth, crime, ecological disarray, the plundering of natural resources, war, alienation, and on and on. But a major ingredient of all these troubled conditions is the clash of human wills or interests or values. When we confront a "social problem," we can be fairly sure that people are at odds about how they would like to see the situation changed. And this realization immediately clouds the prospects for any "rational insight" which might lead to "solution" of the "problems." If societies were really "things," we could locate the offending part and replace it, or redesign and reshape the entire assembly of "parts." But here the "parts" are people and groups, with ideas, needs, interests, values and, above all, plans of their own. These "parts" may not only be disinclined to "behave" as we may want them to; their potentials for action evolve and change constantly in response to changes in the rest of the system—including, above all, changes in understanding. Far from being able to assume that social systems will behave like "things," we must regard them as living, ever-changing systems in which we participate. In the succinct phrase of the comic-strip character Pogo, "We have met the enemy, and he is us."

THE ENDS OF INSIGHT

The doctrines discussed in these chapters have all had to reckon with the conflictual nature of those social conditions which might be considered "ripe for betterment." This they have done with varying candor and directness. The arguments advanced on these issues have, of course, been very disparate, but I think I can identify one common thread in all the approaches. That is a line of reasoning which, in composite, goes much like this: True, troubled social conditions may be surrounded by disagreement as to what exactly would constitute "rational" change. But the insights of social science inquiry can help to transcend such short-sighted squabbles. For behind the contentious reality of the present, there lie possibilities of "better" social relations, of a social world which all concerned could acknowledge as superior. Social science can help move us in the direction of such a world by pointing out the possibilities which it offers, and by demonstrating effective means for realizing such possibilities.

For all of their undoubted merits, none of these arguments wholly fulfills its initial promise. None succeeds in showing how any particular program of social inquiry can overcome the contests of interest constitutive of "social problems." None of them convincingly establishes how any particular kind of insight will necessarily unite people in efforts to realize what they could acknowledge as a preferable situation. In every case, it seems to me, the argument breaks down when it comes to demonstrating a shared *interest* in the "better world" disclosed by superior insight. Such arguments always end up imposing a concept of human "interests" which fails to fit the realities of the interests which people actually pursue.

These shortcomings are most apparent in the technocratic, "social problems" approach which has had so much influence in American sociology. There, social problems—conditions ripe for improvement—are seen as situations which contravene the values and interests of all or nearly all members of society. The role of social science is to expose the "problematic" status of such conditions and to develop techniques for their elimination. Some versions of this approach stress the role of the state in coordinating the attack on "social problems." Other versions, such as that of Merton, seem to leave open the possibility that an informed citizenry may conceive and organize such efforts.

The difficulties with this approach have by now received much discussion. It is simply very difficult to show how people of different social positions can be said to share an interest in the eradication of "social problems." In some cases, what one group regards as "problematic"—e.g., a highly skewed income distribution—may seem no more than fitting to others. Elsewhere, people may agree that a condition or situation is undesirable in itself—e.g., pollution; but here, those who profit from the offending condition will have very different ideas about what constitutes a "satisfactory solution" from those of the rest of the public.

Merton, the most sophisticated writer in this genre, attempts strenuously to show how "social problems" contravene the interests of all members of society. And certainly, we have many conditions which nobody likes in themselves. But to claim that the general public shares an interest in *particular* solutions to these conditions is to impose one's own ideas of what people's interests ought to be over the reality of such interests as they are.

Karl Popper's piecemeal social engineering formula, actually a form of social problems thinking, embodies some very similar difficulties. Popper holds that a "rational" approach to social betterment entails direct attack on human misery, and requires the exclusion of sweeping, theoretically inspired attempts at fundamental social rearrangements. What Popper fails to establish is an effective *community of interest* in eliminating the causes of misery. He naïvely assumes that those with power will find it to their interest to permit social change which gets at the root of misery-producing conditions. Moreover, his insistence on small-scale, incremental efforts at ameliorative change is dogmatic as a general principle. For we have no guarantee that thorough analysis of the causes of misery will not point to really fundamental social conditions as the prime sources of suffering, conditions which people would thus have an interest in changing. Popper's arguments, like Merton's, make sense only if one adopts some artificially restrictive assumptions about the nature of human interests.

Next, consider Gunnar Myrdal's arguments on these subjects. Myrdal acknowledges more directly than do most writers the co-existence of disparate and conflicting value systems, and hence interests, in any society. He also stresses the importance of empirical *beliefs* in orienting everyday social behavior. Many beliefs, he argues, are "opportunistic"—that is, they provide excuses for people to pursue narrow, selfish interests rather than those interests enshrined in people's ultimate valuations. The classical example of this, in Myrdal's writing, is self-serving beliefs among American whites as to the inferiority of blacks. Myrdal's program for social science is to provide authoritative information to drive out the opportunistic beliefs, and thus to change the behaviors stemming from such beliefs. At the same time, where valuations rest on inaccurate beliefs, the social scientist must orient his or her advice to the valuations which people would espouse, were they fully informed.

But Myrdal, too, resorts to unwarranted assumptions about the role of interests in human action. It simply is not true, either in social planning or in everyday life, that destroying a rationalization necessarily changes the behavior being rationalized. Nor does the infusion of new information shape people's pursuit of their interests in wholly predictable ways. People's interests shape their use of information, and do so in ways which cannot necessarily be anticipated in advance. Myrdal too readily assumes that better information will reshape people's preceptions of their interests in what he would consider more "rational" directions.

Similar difficulties assail figures like C. Wright Mills, who address their writings to the needs and perspectives of downtrodden non-elite groups in society. To be sure, writers like Mills cannot be accused of underestimating the advantageousness of "social problems" to particular interests. Their position is that a selfish minority—ordinarily, an exploitative elite—support undesirable conditions such as war or pollution. The role of reasoned social inquiry, by these lights, should be to expose these machinations. This should enable the exploited majority to realize its latent strength and to correct the fundamental causes of the irrational conditions.

But those who advance such arguments are driven to make at least two rather tenuous assumptions about the interests to be set free by these enlightening insights. For one thing, they like to assume that exposing the misery caused to downtrodden groups will spur the majority to sympathy with those groups and to condemnation of their oppressors. But while things may often work this way, we have no guarantee that it must alwýs be so. Fuller information about the plight of homosexuals, for example, however sociologically accurate, may simply strike the public as reasonable and proper.

Another problem is that these critical studies of the short-comings of present social conditions do not necessarily provide blueprints for alternatives. Generally speaking, it is easier to establish consensus that the present scheme of things is unsatisfactory than it is to create unanimity on the shape of a better system. In order to assume that critical insight will necessarily lead to a "more rational" order, Mills or the other exponents of this approach must establish a shared interest in particular forms of social change among all of their "special constituency." And such interests are not easy to demonstrate.

Marxist views on the role of understanding in social betterment encounter analogous difficulties. The more mechanistic Marxist thinkers have tended to place their hopes for significant social betterment on the ultimate and inevitable overthrow of capitalism. But many workers, even those "well enlightened" in Marxist insight, have tended to see their interests, at least for the time being, in the betterment of their position within the capitalist system. The limitations of Marxist notions of interest in this context will receive more discussion below.

Marxists working in the Frankfurt tradition have had to confront another set of ambiguities connected with the notion of interest. Ultimately without faith in the proletariat as a unique force for rationality in modern society, the Frankfurt thinkers have had to reorient their thinking about the interests served by their own activities. They have tended to place their faith in some more diffuse human interest in the improvement of social conditions—a faith in the human capacity for "reason" or "enlightenment," or in what Habermas terms humanity's shared "emancipatory interests." The recourse to such concepts shows an acute sensitivity to the need for some concrete force which could profit from social insight. But none of the Critical Theorists' arguments, including those of Habermas, successfully establish how this diffuse interest in ameliorative change could lead to concrete, working social arrangements which people could acknowledge as "better" than their predecessors.

Thus, the endemic problem of all the approaches considered in this book: how to show that, once duly "enlightened," people will feel an *interest* in acting "rationally." All these writers advance some sort of argument to this point—empirical, sociological accounts of how we can expect people to act. But though any of these accounts may be valid in some circumstances, none is convincing as a *general* account of the relations between insight, interests, and social action.

THE ELUSIVENESS OF HUMAN INTERESTS

The questions raised above suggest an underlying ambiguity in the way we talk about human interests. We speak of interests in at least two senses. Sometimes we talk of interests as inhering a particular social position—e.g., the interests of industrial workers in higher wages and better working conditions. At other times, we reckon interests as those things which people can actually be seen to strive for, as when we note that someone has a self-evinced interest in butterfly collecting or wine connoisseurship. Most of the time, these two ways of talking about interests seem to coexist gracefully. When we see workers striking for higher pay and better working conditions, we draw the comfortable conclusion that they are acting in their interests.

But things get more confusing when people seek ends which strike us as inconsistent with their "natural" or "proper" interests. In such a case, we are apt to conclude that the people have made a "mistake" in their interests—ordinarily because of bad information. Like a ship heading off course, the action in question seems to reflect bad social navigation, something to be corrected by more complete charts or better instruments. When people persist in ignoring their "true interests" despite our best efforts to enlighten them, we are apt to regard them as perverse or even insane.

Perhaps the most famous analysis of the evolution of human interests in shaping social change is that of Marx and Engels. In their view, as we all know, the future of capitalism and indeed the prospects for social betterment were to be determined by the gradual apprehension by workers of their true interests. In the early stages of capitalism, Marx and Engels observed, workers erroneously viewed their interests as lying in accommodation with capital. The ineluctable march of events would show, however, that the gains of the working-class movement within the capitalist system were bound to be short-lived and illusory. Instead, the "mature" working classes would come to see their *ultimate* interests in the destruction of the apparatus of capitalism altogether.

Marx developed lengthy theoretical arguments against the idea that workers had any significant interest in working within the structures of capitalism. He was at great pains to show, for example, how the demands of trade unions could not for any length of time raise the wages of workers. At the same time, Marx and Engels personally campaigned against moderate tendencies in the nascent working-class movement, insisting that "bread and butter" unionism was a cruel hoax, a distraction from workers' true interests.

It is now a commonplace that Marx's predictions about the future of capitalism have not been fulfilled. Capitalism has proved much more flexible in its political and economic institutions than Marx imagined it would, and workers have gradually made significant, if circumscribed, gains in political power and economic well-being. To be sure, the idea of the destruction of capitalism and its replacement by a more rational "workers' state" remains persuasive for many. But probably no one nowadays would deny that workers have been able to pursue certain meaningful interests within the structure of capitalism.

Marx and Engels concluded *The Communist Manifesto* with the ringing appeal, "The proletarians . . . have nothing to lose but their chains." But the authors certainly would have acknowledged that their words were rhetorical flourish; anyone joining a militant social movement has a great deal to lose. In the choice to join in seeking the long-term political interests of people like oneself, one will certainly lose a modicum of comfort and peace of mind, at the very least. Workers in Marx's time who joined such movements stood a good chance of losing even their lives. Strictly speaking, any such appeal to join a collective action is unlikely to amount to an appeal to adopt more effective ways of achieving one's original interests. Instead, it represents an appeal to *redefine* one's personal interests to include pursuit of the well-being of one's class, or of some other larger social grouping or principle. It is not an appeal for a better way of achieving what one already seeks, but an appeal to entertain a somewhat different form of pursuit.

A more recent exploration of human interests in relation to social action is Mancur Olson's justly celebrated book *The Logic of Collective Action.*[1] In this work, Olson, an economist by training, turns his attention to sociological issues. Why, he wonders, do people join and support large-scale social enterprises like political parties, lobbying organizations, and social movements? The usual explanation that the members are seeking to achieve the "collective goods" produced by these bodies leaves Olson skeptical. Why would any particular farmers, for example, support a lobbying group aimed at legislation to improve the lot of all farmers? After all, they would reap the benefits of this particular "collective good" whether they had helped to attain it or not. Olson demonstrates that, when the number of participants is large, the contribution of any one party to a collective action is unlikely to affect that participant's opportunity to enjoy the benefits of the action. All of this leads Olson to conclude that the *inducements to participate* in such activities must be something other than interest in the collective good.

Looking closely at the social organization of some large-scale collective actions of this kind, Olson finds some interesting answers to his questions. Often the leadership of such bodies offers

[1] Cambridge, Mass.: Harvard University Press, 1965.

members special benefits which, unlike the collective goods, can be withheld from non-members. Thus, a labor union may offer its members insurance at preferential rates, or a farmers' lobby special advice and instruction on farming techniques. The result of such measures, Olson argues, is to create an effective *interest* in participation. In the absence of such an interest, would-be members will tend to await the benefits of collective action passively, as "free riders."

Marx and Olson each work with some axiomatic assumptions about human interests—rather different ones, to be sure. For Marx, what one might call the "normal" or "rational" perception of one's interest is the identification of that interest with those of one's class. For Olson, the normal or expected perception of one's interest has to do with pursuit of rewards or gratifications to one's self individually. Marx's view of human interests cannot tell us much about why some workers refractorily pursue narrow individual interests in contrast to class interests, when the opportunities for and inducements to acting on the latter ought to be ample. Neither can Olson's style of analysis tell us much about why people, in the *absence* of selective rewards, do often embrace the blood, sweat, and tears of dedication to a social movement.

It should be obvious that each of these two styles of analysis illuminates major, important categories of social behavior. It would be sterile, I think, to attempt to distinguish which view of human interest represents the more "rational" or more authentic case. The most fruitful use of a comparison like this, it seems to me, is to goad us to account as best we can for the conditions in which each form of interest is liable to emerge as the effective force in social behavior. And if we are prudent, we will not assume that the possibilities here are only twofold.

The trouble, as C. Wright Mills put it, is that people may simply not be *interested* in their interests. Or to be more exact, the interests which social scientists or others might regard as "normal" for the occupants of a given structural position may, in any particular case, prove to be little guide to their actions. The attempt to determine once and for all the "true interests" of any particular category of people is fraught with the temptation to impose one's own preferences in the name of science.

No doubt some deterministic-minded thinkers would insist that people's interests are always knowable *in principle,* if one only had enough data and suitably sophisticated formulae for analyzing them. I have my doubts about this position on logical grounds. People's perceptions of their interests change constantly according to many circumstances, including others' knowledge. Thus, determining the interests of a person or a group at a particular point could, in principle, change the interest itself. But these rather abstract considerations aside, the rigorous determination of what interests people will pursue in any given situation is well beyond the reach of current social science capabilities. We may at best make predictions about what human interests will most likely emerge at particular points. But we would be foolish not to accept evidence that, our predictions notwithstanding, the people in question have evolved some other view of their interests. People's interests do not simply inhere in the nature of the situation in which they find themselves. They emerge and are defined anew in people's every new encounter with their world. Unanticipated definitions of interest cannot necessarily be attributed to misinformation on the part of the people concerned.

By now, some readers will certainly be wondering what all of this has to do with the contribution of insight to social betterment. The answer is, a great deal. I have argued that programs for ameliorative social insight claim, in one way or another, to disclose to people their "true interests" in more harmonious, more productive, more effective or otherwise "more enlightened" patterns of action. But all such arguments, it seems, require that we assume that people will pursue what are considered normal or appropriate "enlightened" interests, once the benefits of widened understanding are conferred. This creates an enormous temptation to regard as "natural" those interests which fit the needs of the theory. And these may not be the interests which people actually do seek.

Consider again the difficulties of Myrdal's position. Myrdal acknowledges that the populations covered by a social planner's schemes may not initially desire the changes which he or she has in mind for them. This candid admission poses problems for Myrdal, since he is committed to developing formulae for enlightenment based on the values of the people concerned. But Myrdal argues that the planner's schemes need not fit people's *present* values—or wishes or interests. They should correspond to what those things *would* be, *if* people were only fully informed of all the relevant facts. Moreover, where present valuations are unfavorable to innovative planning, the planner should be guided by the valuations which people *would have,* once the planned social transformations were complete.

The chances of applying a strategy like this without imposing the planner's own values and interests are nil. Among all the possible "facts" which might be imagined to bear on the reformulation of people's valuations, the researcher will inevitably choose those which, he or she feels, would lead public opinion in the desired direction. Similar convenient conclusions will be drawn in imagining the valuations people would espouse, once the planned-for processes of social change had run their course. The inevitable result of putting these injunctions into effect would be to project a version of the planners' own wishes and interests as those of the people under study. Probably this is pretty much what researchers do when they plan for very sweeping forms of ameliorative social change—they rely on their own image of what is "best" for the people concerned. There is no reason why such an approach need necessarily be selfish or cruel. But it is less than realistic to hold out the hope that such *gedanken* experiments can divine the "real interests" of the people concerned. It amounts to imposing someone else's view of what their interests "ought" to be, and we should recognize it as such.

Still, it is easy to appreciate the temptation to claim that one's programs for understanding do no more than help people pursue their own "true interests." For such a view relieves responsibility for imposing one's own wishes or predilections upon others. Moreover, it makes it easier to claim that the program of enlightenment acts in the interests of "society as a whole." People like the idea that societies as wholes have goals or that troubled social situations display objective requirements for change. If we simply make such convenient assumptions, then giving advice about how to reach such goals incurs no greater responsibility than offering a traveler the best directions one can for reaching the destination of his choice.

The trouble is, the improvement of social conditions can only very rarely be counted a simple means-ends calculation. If someone who must travel from New York to Paris forms the plan of making the trip by car, we can advise him that his interests will be better served by booking a plane or boat. But identifying "interests" in the "improvement" of social situations as wholes usually means addressing situations where people's interests are in conflict. To bring about what we might consider a "more satisfactory" social situation, we usually have little choice but to contemplate either ignoring the interests of some participants or encouraging some or all to redefine their interests. And such advice, though perhaps worthwhile, can hardly be dispassionate or nonpartisan.

But surely, some readers will feel, this argument must have its limits. Let it be agreed, they might say, that "social problems" entail social conflicts; let it be agreed that people will not always pursue what the theorist may regard as their "rational" interests, even after being "duly enlightened." Nevertheless, can't we at least sometimes identify shared interests in certain forms of social improvement? Aren't interests in social harmony at least as real as the conflicting interests which set the stage for social problems? What about a case like the strife-torn situation of the 1970's in Northern Ireland? Surely such agonizing instances of human suffering can be counted irrational and unacceptable from almost any standpoint.

One doubts that the parties to debilitating civil conflicts like those in Northern Ireland find the destruction desirable in itself— any more than anyone finds pollution or poverty a good thing in itself. Probably all concerned would prefer a "solution," if only the solution could be on their terms. Indeed, it is possible that all of the parties would even favor a compromise, yet remain unable to put one into effect. The reasons for this are not really difficult to understand. Sometimes, of course, one or both sides may be dominated by extremists who define any form of compromise as unacceptable to their interests. Elsewhere, however, influential elements on both sides might actually prefer a compromise, if only they could be certain that the other side would keep its side of the arrangement. Unfortunately, the cumulative bitterness and mistrust of civil conflicts often makes such assurance especially difficult. And such uncertainty may play into the hands of very small numbers of extremists, who prefer continued bloodshed to compromise in any event. In agonizing cases like these, people may desire an "alternative" but remain unable to hit upon a *particular* alternative arrangement in which they share an interest.

Such situations have much in common with very destructive but short-lived episodes like panics in burning buildings. There, people may literally trample one another to death in a vain effort to escape, while a "rational effort" to leave the building in an orderly fashion might save lives. People often wonder why reason seems to have failed in these situations. But analysis of the events may show that the quickly emergent structure of the situation did not provide anyone with the choice of opting for such an orderly alternative. The situation faced by each participant in such situations may present only a choice between certain death and a desperate chance at joining the panic. Here again, one could say that the participants had an interest in an "alternative," but had no specific alternative arrangement to opt for.

The idea that people might actually be said to have an "interest" in destructive sequences of action may seem a depressing conclusion indeed. But it is precisely situations like these which may offer social science a chance to contribute to enlightened compromise. For people in protracted conflict situations like the one in Northern Ireland may be especially susceptible to *redefining* their interests in terms of a compromise solution, if only viable terms can be envisaged. Social scientists should be especially qualified to suggest how people might come to prefer an interest, for example, in some guarded form of coexistence rather than in continued strife. What will certainly be needed if such a redefinition is to succeed, and what social science should be able to provide, is some *concrete scenario as to how the newly defined interests will be pursued in specific social arrangements.* A vague "interest" in compromise or coexistence is not enough. Every experienced negotiator will realize that people must believe that such interests can actually form the basis for an alternative way of life. These must be arrangements in which certain minimal requirements on both sides—e.g., freedom of worship for antagonists in communal strife—can be fulfilled. An interest in such concrete compromise should always stand a chance of prevailing against an abstract interest in victory at any price. To be sure, the accumulated mistrust mentioned above will always make such compromise difficult. But the skills of social scientists in designing alternative social arrangements which actually promise to work should give such alternatives their best possible chance for success.

Now, there is nothing remarkable about praising the virtues of compromise, and I would hardly want to claim such praise as the special contribution of this discussion. The special emphasis of these observations is simply as follows: First, no notion of any unique "rational solution" to such dilemmas, or of the correct or "normal" interests of the parties concerned, will be much help in devising compromises like these. Second, virtually any solution will involve redefining the interests of at least some of the participants. And such redefinition always represents the responsibility of whoever proposes it, as an active imposition of his or her interests upon the participants. Happily, most people, most of the time, would probably endorse a redefinition of interests to favor mutual survival over some more parochial political or religious interest.

We might recall here the discussion in Chapter Three of Runciman's advice on how to make one's value positions more attractive to those who espouse contrary values. We could helpfully recast Runciman's remarks in terms of appeals for redefinition of self-interest:

> One tries to secure the approval of someone whose view of his interests seem destructive by conjuring up an alternative view of his interests and of their implementation in practice. Then one tries to get him to see how much more rewarding it would be to pursue the latter, more feasible and less destructive interests than his original interests. "But surely," one would say, "it is more attractive to have a good chance at co-existence with the other group while preserving one's religious identity than to seek total victory at incalculable cost on both sides," or whatever it might be.

Runciman's original proposal is not so very different from the way we do often deal with value differences; as the discussion in Chapter Three noted, we have absolutely no assurance that it will necessarily work. But in conflict situations where survival is perhaps the only shared value, this version of his strategy would seem well worth trying. And we have the best chance to make it work if we forget about what people's interests "ought to be" and concentrate on whatever interpretation of the interests of those concerned promises to stop the situation short of total destruction.

A CHOICE OF WEAPONS

For some readers, to be reduced to considering formulae for compromise may seem tantamount to defeat—or at least, a sorry alternative to the hope for authentic "rational solutions." From this point of view, it no doubt seems perverse to criticize other approaches if one can offer nothing more than compromise in their place.

But I have not categorically denied the usefulness of the various strategies considered in this book. On the contrary, any and all of them may provide important insights, ones which I would value in particular contexts. My criticisms have had to do with the *claims* made for the strategies. None of them, I feel, can justly claim to be a general method. The insights of each are valid only on the fulfillment of certain assumptions. Whether these assumptions hold in any particular instance can only be an empirical question.

Let us consider what we might gain from these approaches in some particular instance. What insights would each impart in regard to enlightened action, say, on slum housing?

What can we learn about dealing with slums, for example, from the Frankfurt tradition? First, the Frankfurt thinkers might ask, is it productive to discuss "policy" in this respect at all, in separation from larger questions of social improvement? May it not be that "policy options" as developed by "experts" themselves embody artificial constraints on "rational choice?" Perhaps accepting these options would represent an implicit denial of some even more profoundly rational alternative. And then, who is to participate in formulating the response to the offending conditions? Whose interests and values will dictate the definition of the "problem," and whose lives will be treated, on the contrary, as "conditions" for manipulation in carrying out the plans? Do the range of possible approaches being considered really include the most fundamental ways of meeting human needs and potentials which the situation permits? Under particular conditions, any of these questions, and many others which might be inspired by the Frankfurt tradition, could yield highly pertinent insights.

These questions would have much in common with those of writers like C. Wright Mills, who address their work to the viewpoint of "outsiders" to power. Like the Frankfurt thinkers, these writers would ask, first of all, what groups in society would benefit from "planning" on slums, and who would lose. How do elite interests in the treatment of slum housing differ from those of the slum dwellers, and from the general public? Could the "true story" of these things unmask the selfish interests of those at the top and arm the hitherto confused public for corrective action? Here, too, particular investigators in particular situations might profit richly from this line of inquiry.

For other purposes, we might find the insights of Sir Karl Popper essential. Is our approach to the offending conditions, he might ask, the most direct attack on human misery that we can imagine under the circumstances? Are the plans for action well precedented, so that their chances of misfiring are minimized? Have the planners been careful not to take unnecessary risks by making the scope of the plans too wide? Or have they taken on social complexities which their understanding does not permit them to handle? All of these questions are worth asking—though not necessarily worth answering in Popper's way.

Similarly, we may derive much from asking questions which Myrdal might formulate. How will the planned response to slum conditions interact with the values and beliefs of the people concerned? How will values and beliefs differ according to the different categories of people involved? Do people in the groupings involved believe that change is desirable or even possible where slums are concerned? Must beliefs or values change before any social changes can take place? Can social science play a role in such changes? Which valuations and beliefs in the situation might provide a basis for action on the social scientist's insights, and which will tend to block such action?

Finally, we can even profit from the insights of the social problem solvers, provided that we use their approach as a series of questions rather than as a series of answers. We might ask, for example, how much consensus we can build as to what steps represent a "reasonable solution" to the "slum problem." We might even attempt to broaden this consensus by adducing sociological arguments as to the injuriousness of slum conditions. I doubt that such consensus can ever embrace all the different social groups

concerned in any significant social problem. But this approach may
at least help organize the thinking of like-minded antagonists of
offending conditions. And once a desire for change is crystallized,
social science may contribute by helping to assess the likely results
of different actions to "cure" the problem. Provided that the limits of consensus are acknowledged and the political content of such
plans recognized, this approach may prove quite useful to the participants in it.

Any of these perspectives, then, may set off a fruitful line of inquiry for a particular thinker. But for another investigator, or for
the same investigator in another setting, the given approach may
prove irrelevant and misleading. The utility of each of these strategies, it seems to me, depends on two things. First, on the basic political orientation of the thinker—that is, both upon ultimate values and upon those "articles of faith" which represent working
assumptions about social change. Second, upon the possibilities and
constraints which the empirical realities of the situation under consideration seems to exhibit. Obviously, the second is bound in prac
tice to be colored by the first, though in principle we ought to be
able to distinguish, say, between when a situation is resistant to
change and when it is the investigator who is resistant.

But none of these strategies can possibly hold for the whole
range of value perspectives, and the whole range of empirical possibilities of situations "ripe for change." This conclusion is nothing if not consistent with the detailed criticisms of the various
approaches offered in the preceding chapters. For again, I have argued not that the perspectives were useless, but that they embodied
weighty political assumptions which could not be accepted *a priori*.

Once again, then, we confront the fundamental "ideological"
assumptions which orient all social inquiry. Much as it would sim-
plify things to find a way of dealing "rationally" with social conditions which bypassed these fundamental questions, the hope of
doing so is vain. Such orienting assumptions about what is possible
and desirable in social change enter into every consideration of
the subject.

I have argued that such assumptions, including value differences, are subject to a measure of reasoned debate. The content of such assumptions is partly empirical, and to this extent the methods of social science may at least narrow the range of disagreement. Many debates over political values, for example, are largely disputes over the *effects* of putting different principles into practice. Does participatory democracy really suffice to organize the decision making of a social movement? Would a social system survive if the state were to foreswear the use of coercion? Further, many political doctrines are predicated on empirical assumptions about the origins of present conditions—e.g., the assumption that bad aspects of the present system result from the machinations of a selfish elite. Here, too, social science methods can help evaluate such assumptions.

Still, the limitations of this approach are very severe. A major ingredient of the feasibility of different political and social forms, as we have seen, is people's belief in that feasibility. Moreover, the empirical questions involved in disputes between fundamental political and social viewpoints are typically so diffuse and multifaceted as to resist any straightforward resolution. Certainly, we ought to try to wear away at the empirical elements of these fundamental differences. But we need not expect to bring these questions to a quick or decisive resolution.

We would do well to remember the very multiplicity of disparate but entirely feasible plans for ordering social relations. Purist adherents of different political, social, or religious values are apt to complain that the virtues of their beliefs would be apparent to all, if only they could receive a "fair chance"—that is, if only people made one wholehearted attempt to make them work. To this we might observe that all sorts of different values or scenarios for social life might "work," given general cooperation with them. But such widespread willingness to make any particular plan work is a great rarity.

Those who propose strategies for improving social relations usually entertain some model of the "improved" social system to

result. They assume, as I have argued, that if people are "enlightened" as to the true potential of this new order, they will tend to
strive to realize it. These assumptions are most blatant in functionalist arguments, but are by no means confined to them. The
trouble is that those at whom the enlightenment is directed may
well be entertaining other equally vivid models of how society
could be better. In some sense, many of these models might stand
a good chance of working—again, if only all concerned would give
them a "fair try."

Social systems, whatever their systemic qualities, differ from or-
ganisms in one fundamental respect. Their parts—people—can be
radically changed in their relations to one another, can change their
"functions," without suffering much wear or tear. Entire spheres
of social activity can be suppressed—indeed, the unit can even
break down into smaller units—and the people concerned can
still survive and flourish. Given that this is so, the range of "feasible alternatives" in social life is in principle vast.

Understanding these things should sharpen our appreciation of
the importance of program and prognosis, the concepts developed
by Myrdal and Streeten. The implication of these ideas is that
people's views of the nature of social relations interact continu-
ously with their plans and desires for social change. Moreover, as
Streeten points out, other people's programs help form the basis
for one's own prognoses and hence affect one's own programs. We
may prefer to think about social relations as "things," whose potential roles in future social change are fixed. But Myrdal and
Streeten remind us that those potentials for change are themselves
subject to continual reformulation, as ideas of what is possible in
social life—prognoses—and how the possible is to be transformed
into the actual—programs—themselves change. Given the diversity of social arrangements which are theoretically "feasible"—
provided that people believe in them—the interaction of program
and prognosis takes on great importance in setting the limits of
social change.

The fluidity of judgments as to what forms of change one may "reasonably" hope and plan for leads to some agonizing social choices. These choices are extremely difficult to reduce to "rational" formulae. Consider, for example, a split between moderates and militants in a left-wing political party over the party's possible participation in reformist policies. The militants, let us suppose, refuse any support for such measures. They contend that the reforms do not go nearly far enough, and that any left-wing participation in such inadequate measures will defuse working-class support for more sweeping changes. The moderates, let us suppose, concede the preferability of sweeping over modest changes, but claim that the former are impossible "under present circumstances." Given the present weakness of the left, the moderates may contend, half a loaf is surely preferable to none.

The militants may accuse their former allies of not really sharing their radical values. This may in any specific case be true, but we cannot dismiss the possibility that the moderates simply are responding to a different reading of the possibilities of the situation. Yet, the effect of the moderates' cooperation in reformist plans may well be to make the militants' predictions come true. Thus, a situation is created where parties with the same values, and diagnoses of the present situation which differ perhaps only in degree, adopt diametrically opposed courses of action. Spokesmen for both parties, if asked, will no doubt defend their decisions as the only "rational" choice.

Anyone attentive to social processes knows that situations like this are by no means confined to left-wing politics, or indeed to politics in general. It is a durable irony of social life that otherwise small differences in social prognoses can lead to the most bitterly antagonistic choices for action. And the role of the decision maker is not only a passive one, for decisions as to the "possibilities of the situation" also help to constitute those possibilities. The militant political faction may hope that, through the left's withholding support from reformist measures, such measures will ultimately fail. They may concede that dissatisfaction with the policies of the center are not yet sufficient to give the left a chance; but they will contend that the left's definition of reform as hopeless will ultimately assure its hopelessness. Such gambits do often bear fruit— in politics and in the rest of life. But then, the moderates' scenario often comes true, as well, and not only because they make it come true. The most vociferous left-wing criticism of "muddling through" with piecemeal measures does not assure the failure of such measures. The majority who occupy the middle ground have their own programs and prognoses, and these, too, help shape the ultimate outcomes of events.

I have often wondered whether mathematical models or computer simulations could yield unique "rational decisions" for choices like these under specified conditions. But whether or not this is possible in theory, I doubt that such precise determinations could ever be made in the real world. For in real choice situations, where the conditions of choice are others' constantly changing programs and prognoses, exogenous forces continually intrude to reshape the situation for all concerned. A key participant dies, the economy improves or falls apart, someone's mistress takes her story to the newspapers—or, most unaccountably of all, a new generation grows up who simply entertain different programs and prognoses from its predecessor. Thus, I argue that even the most intelligent decision making in these highly fluid situations must entail a measure of faith. And while empirical analysis can distinguish between plausible articles of faith and the really farfetched, there will always be plenty of room for dispute among equally plausible assumptions.

The implications of all this for rational social decision making are many, though hardly simplifying. These reflections should remind us, for example, how difficult it is even to establish on rational grounds the "options for choice" inherent in a situation. The fact that the people in question may recognize few possibilities for change or none at all hardly excuses the concerned student from considering wider possibilities. The community organizer may arrive in a new neighborhood to find community members dispirited, convinced that nothing can be done to improve their situation. The organizer, who must also be a social analyst, may well believe that much is possible, if only the residents will believe it possible. But how great a change in the situation is it reasonable and conscientious to entertain? Is it more "rational" and more responsible to seek fundamental or piecemeal change? Given that the community organizer no doubt intends to add his or her hopes to the new prognoses for a better situation, how sweeping is he or she entitled to make these new prognoses?

Popper was right to underline the extreme importance, in social planning, of the scope and time perspective of ameliorative plans. But he was wrong to argue that plans for far-reaching and fundamental social rearrangements must always be irrational. True, big plans do entail the risk of running up against big and badly understood countervailing forces. But then, small plans run the risk of being thwarted by fundamental contextual forces which only respond to holistic, forceful planning. Which danger one counts more serious depends on one's own values and on one's diagnosis of the possibilities of the situation under consideration. And the analysis of such possibilities shows that they consist largely of expressions of "faith" which are continually being revised—both one's own articles of faith and those of the people who comprise the situation. The indeterminacy which all this implies should counsel caution in the formulation of all sorts of "rational" social plans.

"THE SOLUTION" OR "A FIGHTING CHANCE"?

Again, some readers may find in these guarded remarks confirmation of their initial suspicions. "Sure enough," they are saying, "the writer has no solution of his own." And indeed, I oppose the idea of "a solution" in the sense of a program of social inquiry to fit all social realities and all investigators' value dispositions. It strikes me that the search for such a "solution" has often distracted good minds from promising possibilities of less grandiose contributions to enlightening insight. For I hold that most social situations offer significant openings for insight to play a useful role. And though we have no certainty of success, and indeed no certainty that we could agree on the meaning of "success," we have at least a fighting chance of making a contribution. Surely that chance is worth taking. And we will make the most of it if we renounce any idea of a comprehensive "solution" to the "problem of rational social betterment."

Surely the view that there must be a unique "rational solution" to questions like these is a historical phenomenon. Sir Isaiah Berlin has identified some similar ideas as crystallizing in the rationalism of the nineteenth century. He writes:

> Conservatives, liberals, radicals, socialists differed in their interpretation of historical change. They disagreed about what were the deepest needs, interests, ideals of human beings, about who held them, and how deeply or widely or for what length of time, about the method of their discovery, or their validity in this or that situation. They differed about the facts, they differed about ends and means, they seemed to themselves to agree on almost nothing. But what they had in common—too obviously to be fully aware of it themselves—was the belief that their age was ridden with social and political problems which could be solved only by the conscious application of truths upon which all men endowed with adequate mental powers could agree.[2]

Berlin's view is that this conviction has brought about much mischief. He summarizes what he sees as the essence of this "rationalistic bias" as follows:

> . . . first, that all men have one true purpose, and one only, that of rational self-direction; second, that the ends of all ra-

[2] *Four Essays on Liberty* (New York: Oxford University Press, 1970), pp. 12–13.

tional beings must of necessity fit into a single universal, harmonious pattern, which some men may be able to discern more
clearly than others; third, that all conflict, and consequently
all tragedy, is due solely to the clash of reason with the irrational or the insufficiently rational . . . ; finally, that when
all men have been made rational, they will obey the rational
laws of their own natures, which are one and the same in them
all, and so be at once wholly law-abiding and wholly free.[3]

This view is all the more dangerous, in Berlin's estimation for being fundamentally misguided:

If, as I believe, the ends of men are many, and not all of them
are in principle compatible with each other, then the possibility
of conflict—and of tragedy—can never wholly be eliminated
from human life, either personal or social. The necessity of
choosing between absolute claims is then an inescapable characteristic of the human condition. This gives its value to freedom as Acton had conceived of it—as an end in itself, and not
as a temporary need. . . .[4]

Note that Berlin does not argue that human ends—he also
might have said human interests or values—must necessarily conflict with one another. Still less does he suggest that human institutions may never manage to coordinate such ends smoothly. Berlin says, rather, that we cannot afford to *assume* that human ends
or interests must necessarily always be compatible with one another. Nor should we hope to discover or deduce some unique
"rational model" of what such ends should always be. Attempts to
develop such models in the name of reason, and subsequent efforts
to fit people's lives to the procrustian form of such models, have
brought about much grief. Our best hope, Berlin seems to be saying, lies not in seeking a single optimal vision of what human nature is and what social life ought to be. Instead, we should attempt
to develop social arrangements as accommodating and as responsive as possible to the seemingly endless variation in human ends.

[3] Ibid., p. 154.
[4] Ibid., p. 169.

The message of this book, it seems to me, has much in common with Berlin's conclusions. Nothing justifies our assuming the existence of a single "rational solution" to any distressed social situation, or of "true ultimate interests" of the parties to it. We can and should offer our insights for the improvement of social conditions. But we must assume that the insight, and the effects which we intend for it, are specific to our own values and to our diagnoses of the possibilities of the situation.

From my own value standpoint, I would prefer that programs of rational enlightenment be organized as attacks on "the causes of human misery," though with the assumption that not all forms of misery need entail conscious physical suffering. The term, of course, comes from Barrington Moore, though Popper invokes much the same language. More like Moore than like Popper, however, I feel that such attacks must be oriented to fundamental structural conditions in society having key roles in generating misery. This assumption immediately throws discussion into the thick of political analysis as to what those conditions may be, and which of them are susceptible to change. So far as I am concerned, major causes of much actual and potential misery in advanced industrial societies, in principle susceptible to enlightened change, are the vast inequities in wealth and power in these societies.

If one is to consider a specific program of rational enlightenment to address this or any other social prognosis, one must immediately ask how people's interests might be reformulated so that the desired changes might come about. And seeking a redefinition of people's interests can mean anything from threatening their lives to subjecting them to suasions like those adapted above from Runciman. Personally, my valuation is for less coercive alternatives; I feel that misery brought about by forcing large numbers of people to be different can easily outweigh the gains. But we should not delude ourselves; moderation, too, can have its costs. One can always imagine extreme situations which would test one's own or others' aversion to coercion.

Perhaps the important point is that the reformulations of interest which insight may seek to foster vary widely in their humaneness. I am happiest with those forms of insight and advice which elicit people's active responses to the reinterpretations of interest recommended to them. Indeed, realizing that possibilities for social change are largely constituted by the prognoses which people carry in their heads suggests to me the wisdom of letting change in prognoses precede and help shape changes in behavior.

Thus, we can leave much room for people's reactions to our advice and insight, and we can minimize coercion in the changes we advocate. But we cannot hope to leave any social situation where we offer insight untouched by the force of our own guiding interests. We must renounce forever the possibility of social amelioration through administration of "technical judgments," to use Merton's terms. If people's "ultimate interests" cannot be known, it remains for us to support those interests which we regard as most worthy and as most feasible under the circumstances. I simply hope that most people would share the concern with reducing human misery as a key guiding interest for social inquiry.

Acknowledging these things should sharpen our appreciation of the responsibility borne by anyone providing understanding to bear on the improvement of social conditions. The needs or requirements of such situations never speak for themselves. The investigator, if his or her advice has any impact at all, always helps to shape the perceptions of the interests of those concerned. Even the range of "options for choice" seemingly inherent in the situation must receive critical examination by the investigator. He or she must decide, given what he or she has defined as the "needs" of the people concerned, how profound a change is called for. And this means, among other things, assessing what conditions one can reasonably expect to be changed through insight or persuasion, and which are better left unchanged. Such decisions inevitably engage not only the ultimate values of the thinker, I have argued, but also certain "articles of faith" which are subtle but immensely influential in any rational approach to social change.

It may seem strange that this examination of the possibilities for rational insight on social improvement concludes with an emphasis on such a seemingly non-rational notion as "faith." But it should be apparent that what I have in mind is not simply "blind faith," not a purely irrational or non-rational choice. As Chapter Six argued, reliance on some measure of faith represents an essential ingredient of all social behavior. The very business of carrying out social inquiry implies faith in the social effects of such insight. And such faith can never amount to certainty. We cannot absolutely assure ourselves, for example, that the products of social research will not meet with predominantly destructive or exploitative uses. We may control the "production" of such insight, insofar as we ourselves are the producers, but we cannot ordinarily control its "consumption." Innovations in social understanding may lead to cruel uses of even those insights gathered with the most benign intent. The course of technological development, including the technology of behavior control, is predictably unpredictable in these respects.

Based on these observations, arguments can be advanced against *all* forms of social inquiry, either that directed at social betterment or any other. According to these arguments, the risk that social understanding may be put to destructive ends is so great that we would be better off not to make such understanding available. Such arguments are not to be dismissed out of hand, especially given the unprecedented powers for manipulation conferred by modern technologies. It seems to me, for example, that we ought to consider limiting the development of those forms of knowledge which lend themselves especially directly to human destructiveness— both in social and natural science.

But a limit on social scientists' studies of ameliorative possibilities for social change strikes me as self-defeating. For those determined to perfect means for social manipulation will likely remain undeterred by such injunctions within the scientific community. Working social scientists sincerely concerned with social betterment ought to have a chance to act as counterweights to their more manipulative counterparts. Yet no program can *guarantee* such happier results. We can do no better than to place educated faith in the pursuit of those insights which strike us as most promising.

What, then, is my own program for social inquiry? I have no "program" to offer, but rather a way of going at programs like those discussed in this book. My own value preferences are for the most candid possible admission of the investigator's own role in shaping events through infusion of "rational insight." And as I have said, I prefer those forms of insight which shift people's perceptions of their interest by persuasion rather than by coercion. I do not see how such fundamental presuppositions as these can be fully justified through any logical process. But I do believe that most people would join me in preferring these choices, given the fullest understanding of the effects of doing so, compared with the effects of adopting other approaches.

Beyond this, I believe that we can do no better than to pursue those programs of enlightenment which strike us as most urgently needed. This will probably mean relying on some version of one of the approaches discussed in this book—and probably on different ones of these in different situations. We can do these things more honestly, and indeed more effectively, if we remain sensitive to the limitations of each of the approaches discussed here. We should match the techniques which we adopt to our own values and to our interpretations of the possibilities of the situations which we confront. And as we do these things, we ought, at least by my lights, to be as open as possible about the assumptions which we invoke in doing so.

We need have no illusions that the results of our studies will necessarily be consistent with one another. On the contrary, we should prepare ourselves for all sorts of disagreements. But we need not regard such disputes as final; instead, they represent an opportunity for a more refined attack on the issues in question. When we disagree, we ought first to attend to the content of our differences. In cases where such differences arise from different interpretations of empirical material, we can focus scholarly debate on those differences. Elsewhere, the differences will stem either from what I have termed discrepant "articles of faith," or from differences of ultimate value. We can at least do our best to get these differences out in the open and trace their effects. Some such differences, I have argued, embody empirical elements, and those empirical aspects provide a chance for rational narrowing of differences.

Sometimes differences over rational steps for social improvement will seem irreconcilable through rational means. Then we must contemplate some formula for compromise. Sometimes the value of survival will be all that the parties have in common; indeed we cannot be certain that they will always have that much. Perhaps the best we can do here is to discount any formula for a "rational solution" independent of what the parties are prepared to live with.

Finally, we have to tell the truth. Sometimes social inquiry will lead to insights or findings which we find distasteful, or worse. We have to be ready to acknowledge these things in our own work, and grant them a hearing when they are asserted by others, no matter how badly they accord with our values or expectations. "The materialist interpretation of history," Max Weber wrote, "is no cab to be taken at will." The same has to be said for empirical inquiry into possibilities for social change. Once we set off in search of the truth, in hopes of enhancing what we see as the best possibilities of social life, we cannot consistently distort or suppress ideas which displease us. Social inquiry, either that oriented to social betterment or any other, makes no sense unless open to all sorts of information—both the welcome and expected and all the rest. We can take no satisfaction in pursuing uplifting insights unless we are also prepared to deal with the others.

Index